The Islands

Skye, the Hebrides and Arran

The author and publisher have made every effort to ensure that the information in this publication is accurate, and accept no responsibility whatsoever for any loss, injury or inconvenience experienced by any person or persons whilst using this book.

published by
pocket mountains ltd
6 Church Wynd, Bo'ness EH51 0AN
www.pocketmountains.com

ISBN: 0-9544217-4-4

A catalogue record for this book is available from the British Library

Printed in Poland

Introduction

This guide contains forty circular routes in the Islands off the West Coast of Scotland. The islands featured in this book include Arran, Islay, Jura, Mull, Eigg, Rum, Skye, Raasay, Harris and the Uists.

Routes have been chosen according to a number of factors, including variety of terrain, great views, historical interest, minimal road walking and the feasibility of a circular route.

Environmental factors such as the ability of access points to support additional cars and opportunities for bypassing visitor-sensitive or eroded areas have also been taken into account. Circular routes help to take the pressure off badly eroded paths, and walking in areas where there have been fewer footsteps is more conducive to natural regeneration of the land.

Walkers can also minimise their own impact on the environment by keeping to purpose-built paths whenever possible and walking in single file to help prevent widening scars. Restricting your use of bikes to tracks, parking sensibly, avoiding fires and litter, and keeping dogs on a lead, particularly on grazing land and during lambing, all help to preserve the land and good relations with its inhabitants. Many of the responsibilities for walkers are now enshrined in law.

How to use this guide

The routes in this book are divided into five regions. These relate to the geographical distribution of the West Coast islands. The opening section for each of the five regions introduces an island or island group and its key features, and contains brief route outlines. It is supplemented by a regional map, locating the walks.

Extra planning is required to access these routes if travelling from the mainland. Caledonian MacBrayne runs the majority of West Coast ferries, but there are also smaller ferry service providers.

Each route begins with an introduction identifying the names and heights of significant tops, the relevant Ordnance Survey (OS) or Harvey map, total distance and average time.

A sketch map shows the main topographical details of the area and the route. The map is intended only to give the reader an idea of the terrain, and should not be followed for navigation.

Every route has an estimated round-trip time: this is for rough guidance only and should help in planning, especially when daylight hours are limited. In winter or after heavy rain, extra time should also be added for difficulties underfoot.

Risks and how to avoid them

Many of the hills in this guide are remote and craggy, and the weather in Scotland can change suddenly, reducing visibility to several yards. Winter walking brings particular challenges, including limited daylight, white-outs, cornices and avalanches. Every year, walkers and climbers die from falls or hypothermia in the Scottish mountains. Equally, though, overstretched Mountain Rescue teams are often called out to walkers who are simply tired or hungry.

Preparation for a walk should begin well before you set out, and your choice of route should reflect your fitness, the conditions underfoot and the regional weather forecasts.

None of the walks in this guide should be attempted without the relevant OS Map or equivalent at 1:50,000 (or 1:25,000) and a compass. In the Cuillin of Skye, the Harvey's map at 1:25,000 and 1:12,500 is advised.

Even in summer, warm, waterproof clothing is advisable and footwear that is comfortable and supportive with good grips a must. Don't underestimate how much food and water you need and remember to take any medication required, including reserves in case of illness or delay. Many walkers also carry a whistle, first aid kit and survival bag.

It is a good idea to leave a route description with a friend or relative in case a genuine emergency arises: you should not rely on a mobile phone to get you out of difficulty. If walking as part of a group, make sure your companions are aware of any medical conditions, such as diabetes, and how to deal with problems that may occur.

There is a route for most levels of fitness in this guide, but it is important to know your limitations. Even for an experienced walker, colds, aches and

pains can turn an easy walk into an ordeal.

These routes assume some knowledge of navigation in the hills with use of map and compass, though these skills are not difficult to learn. Use of Global Positioning System (GPS) devices is becoming more common but, while GPS can help pinpoint your location on the map in zero visibility, it cannot tell you where to go next.

Techniques such as scrambling or climbing on rock are required on many routes in this guide. In severe winters, techniques on snow and ice will also be necessary. Such skills will improve confidence and the ease with which any route can be completed. They will also help you to avoid or escape potentially dangerous areas if you lose your way. The Mountaineering Council of Scotland provides training and information, or you may wish to hire a local guide.

Access

Until the Land Reform (Scotland) Act was introduced early in 2003, the 'right to roam' in Scotland was a result of continued negotiations between government bodies, interest groups and landowners.

In many respects, the Act simply reinforces the strong tradition of public access to the countryside of Scotland for recreational purposes. However, a key difference is that under the Act the right of access depends on whether it is exercised responsibly.

Landowners also have an obligation not

to unreasonably prevent or deter those seeking access. The responsibilities of the public and land managers are set out in the Scottish Outdoor Access Code.

At certain times of the year there are special restrictions, both at low level and on the hills, and these should be respected. These often concern farming, shooting and forest activities: if you are in any doubt, ask. Signs are usually posted at popular access points with details: there should be no expectation of a right of access to all places at all times.

The right of access does not extend to use of motor vehicles on private or estate roads.

Seasonal restrictions

Red and Sika deer stalking:
Stags: 1 July to 20 October
Hinds: 21 October to 15 February
Deer may also be culled at other times for welfare reasons. The seasons for Fallow and Roe deer (less common) are also longer. Many estates belong to the Hillphones network which provides advance notice of shoots.

Grouse shooting:
12 August to 10 December

Forestry:
Felling: all year
Planting: November to May

Heather burning:
September to April

Lambing:
March to May (Dogs should be kept on a lead at all times near livestock.)

Glossary

Common Gaelic words found in the text and maps:

abhainn	river
ailean	field; grassy plain
àirigh	summer hill pasture; shieling
allt	burn; stream
àth	ford
bàn	white
beag	small
bealach	pass; gap; gorge
beinn	ben; mountain
bràighe	neck; upper part
cìoch	breast; hub; pointed rock
clach	boulder; stone
cnoc	hillock
coire	corrie; cauldron; mountain hollow
creachann	exposed rocky summit
creag	cliff
cruach	heap; stack
dubh	black; dark
eilean	island
garbh	thick; coarse; rough
lagan	hollow; dimple
learg	hillside exposed to sea or sun
lochan	small loch; pool
meall	mound; lump; bunch
mór	big; great; tall
sgòrr	peak; cliff; sharp point
sgùrr	large conical hill
stùc	pinnacle; precipice; steep rock

5

Lewis, Harris, the Uists and a host of smaller islands that form the long wedge of the Outer Hebrides have a geographic diversity and wildness of terrain second to none. Long beaches of crushed shell welcome the Atlantic surf, but the only crowds on these shores are the flocks of birds that come to make their winter homes. The hinterland is a maze of machair and lochans, with bogs as porous as sponge. From these flatlands rise the mountains: craggy, savage and unfrequented. The islands are well served by ferries from Ullapool, Skye and Oban, and there are also several air routes.

This section features five routes on Harris, the most mountainous of all these islands. A grand tour of Clisham, the highest in the Outer Hebrides, takes the rocky crescent around the River Scaladale. Two routes enter the high hills from Loch a'Siar to walk above the parallel glens of Meavaig and Chliostair with their intimidating buttresses and craggy tops. A walk along a nature trail starts close to Tarbert to climb a single peak. The fifth and easiest route on Harris begins near the port of Leverburgh. On North Uist, one route navigates the waterscape of Eaval. South Uist contains two routes: a long journey over Hecla and Beinn Mhór traverses some of the most arduous terrain in Britain; and a short escape into the low hills of Lochboisdale completes the set.

Isle of Lewis
Stornoway

North Harris
Taransay
Tarbert
Scalpay

Pabbay
Berneray
South Harris

Sound of Harris

North Uist
Lochmaddy

Benbecula

South Uist
Lochboisdale

Sound of Barra
Eriskay
Barra
Castlebay

6

The Outer Hebrides

The Clisham

An Clisham Ⓒ (799m),
Mulla-Fo-Dhaes (743m)

Walk time 6h40 Height gain 1200m
Distance 17km OS Map Landranger 14

Multiple summits with plenty of ascent and complex ground on a rocky ridge. Some high mountain paths and a good track to return.

Start at the sign for the Frith Rathaud (Harris Way), 800m south of the Scaladale Centre (GR186096). (Good roadside parking.) The sign marks the start of a renovated track, once the postal route to Tarbert from Stornoway. After a gentle southwards climb for about 1.5km, the track takes you to a bealach with a bench and lochan. Leave the track here to bear westwards across bog: complex knolls make for a tough ascent to reach the better slopes of Tomnaval's east ridge. Climb this to the top, which is marked by a cairn. Descend on the west side and begin the steep slopes of An Clisham. Take these directly up the eastern face, where a band of crags at the top can be easily breached to reach the rocky summit (GR155073) (3h). The ridge around Loch Vistem is a great experience, with views to all sides and some exposure over steep drops. To

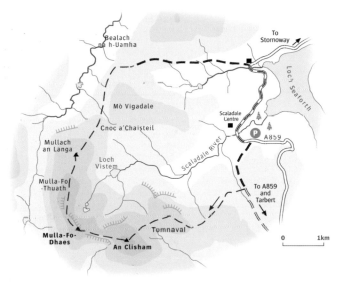

descend, hop north over jagged boulders for 200m before the west ridge takes you more easily down to a bealach. Climb several small knolls before the craggy Mulla-Fo-Dhaes. This can be taken direct on its ridge or along an exposed path on the northern side to reach the summit. Drop northwards from the top and climb Mulla-Fo-Thuath, passing a noticeable band of quartz en route to the steep craggy top. Descend north through awkward boulderfields, keeping close to the steep eastern corrie to reach another bealach. Continue over Mullach an Langa and drop steeply over grass and scree to Cnoc a'Chaisteil, a boggy bealach. Rather than climb Mò Vigadale, contour NNE over boggy ground to gain Bealach na h-Uamha after 1km. Follow an excellent grassy track east from here to the main road at Bàgh Vigadale. Walk south along the road back to the start (6h40).

The Gatliff hostels

Assistant Secretary in the Treasury, Herbert Gatliff was closely linked to the development of the many outdoor access movements in the 1930s, including the National Trust, Youth Hostel Association (YHA) and the Ramblers Association. A frequent visitor to the Hebrides, he decided to set up hostels on the Western Isles where the YHA had no base. There are currently Gatliff hostels at Reinigeadal, Howmore, Berneray and Garenin.

◂ Rainbow from the Scaladale River

Mighty cliffs of Sron Ulladale

Tirga Mór (679m)

Walk time **5h20** Height gain **700m**
Distance **14km** OS Map **Landranger 13**

A single peak reached by good paths and tracks with easy height gain. This route involves limited exposure and some tricky navigation.

Start from the track for the power station just before the sign for Abhainn Suidhe on the B887 along Loch a Siar (GR052078). (Limited parking here.) Take the track northwards over the brow of the hill and down to Loch Leòsaid. Just before a bridge, leave the track and bear northwest to follow the Abhainn Leòsaid on vague tracks.

Cross this burn near some ruins, and then keep to an excellent path above the east bank of the ravine. Follow the path for 2km along the glen to reach a bealach marked with a cairn and great views to the west. Leave the path here, and tramp northwards over the moor. The ground soon becomes firm underfoot, leading to terraces beneath the pink, iron-rich buttresses of Ceartaval. Instead of climbing this hill, bear northeast past Loch Bràigh Bheagarais and make your way up to the bealach of the same name. Turn southwards to climb at first over grass before breaking through a line of boulders and crags. The ridge gains definition higher up, with steep drops to the west, and

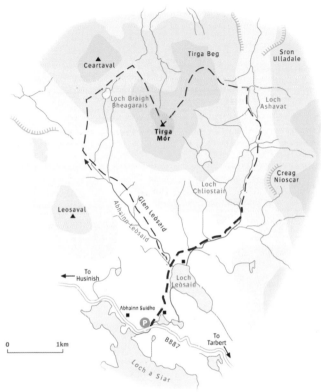

culminates in a long and exposed fin that leads to the summit of Tirga Mór and its mossy trig point (GR055115) (3h). Descend northeast, passing over boulders to reach easier undulating ground. Climb over a knoll and continue northwards for 500m, descending easy grass slopes towards Tirga Beg. Drop eastwards in a gentle arc to follow uneven slopes and watercourses: this descent gives a splendid view of Sron Ulladale, which boasts one of the most intimidating crags in Britain. At the head of Loch Ashavat, you will meet a good path: follow it south down to Loch Chliostair. The dam at the foot of this loch is served by a track that leads back to the start (5h20).

◄ Looking to the peaks of North Harris across the Sound of Taransay

11

High on Harris

Uisgnaval Mór (729m),
Teilesval (697m)

Walk time 5h Height gain 900m
Distance 12km OS Map Landranger 14
or 13

A varied walk, mostly off path, to climb two high peaks with great views and a distinct sense of remoteness.

Start at a bridge at the head of Loch Meavaig on the B887 (GR101063). (Various parking places.) Walk northeast from the east side of the bridge to follow the left side of a fence over boggy terrain. Where the fence ends, maintain your course, climbing over rough terrain to meet the Abhainn Unasta. Follow the burn with its many rapids eastwards to reach flatter ground above. At the point where the burn takes you north near a set of steep crags, leave the water and climb east along a steep heather runnel to gain the ridge by Creag na Speireig. This takes you north over firm ground, gaining height rapidly. Further up, the spur becomes less featured until the eastern corrie opens up with steep drops. The summit of Uisgnaval Mór is set on an exposed crag (GR121086) (2h40). Walk north for 30m from the summit to avoid crags, and then begin a northeasterly descent over scree and grass to reach a prominent bealach shared with Teilesval.

Climb northeast, darting through jagged boulders, to reach the striated bands of rock that mark the summit. Descend north along the main ridge for 500m, easily negotiating boulder-strewn zones to reach a broad spur bearing northwest. Follow this as it evens off and loses definition as it falls again.

Drop westwards into Glen Uisletter at any convenient point opposite the imposing peak of Sron Scourst, and descend over folding but uncomplicated terrain to reach a good track along Glen Meavaig. Follow the track south, past Loch Scourst and back to the start (5h).

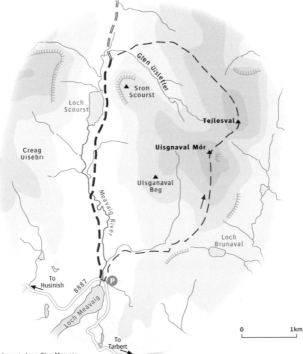

◀ Sron Scourst above Glen Meavaig

Road to Reinigeadal

Toddun (528m)

Walk time **6h** Height gain **600m**
Distance **17km** OS Map Landranger **14**

**One peak with a steep ridge and
some intricate route-finding but good
paths to approach and return. The start
point is within walking distance of
Tarbert, but this route can also be
accessed from Reinigeadal Youth
Hostel or from a parking area above
Loch Maaruig.**

Start at a parking bay just after the
Laxadale Lochs on the road to Scalpay,
3km east of Tarbert (GR184005). Take a
good footpath, signposted for the Gatliff

Youth Hostel at Reinigeadal, to rise slowly
eastwards through the moor. After a large
cairn at a bealach, begin a clever zigzag
descent through bracken to reach a bridge
at the shore of Loch Trollamarig. Follow the
coastal path east to gain height, crossing a
second bridge and ignoring a minor path
just after it. Where the path starts to
descend by some barrel-shaped rocks, leave
it and ascend northwards over heather and
rocks. Cross a tight ravine, not a difficult
obstacle and often dry, to gain the
prominent southeast ridge of Toddun with
its many folds and ribs. Climb steep heather
and slabs to reach the crest of the spur. The
ridge is followed easily, then narrows higher

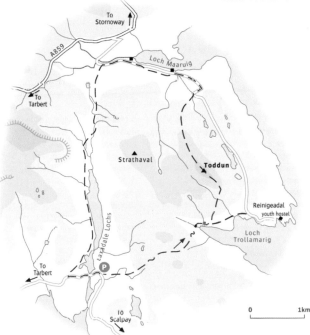

up before easing towards the summit (GR210029) (3h). Descend NNW over the grassy slopes of Cadhan Dubha. Lower down, the ridge turns to complex bumps and boggy stretches. Keep bearing north, ignoring the folds that try to trick you westwards. Aim for a switchback in the road on the east side to avoid the lower fenced fields. Descend along the road towards Loch Maaruig to reach a house at Eilean Anabaich with two very odd windows. To avoid a short road walk, watch for two gates

on the left 60m from the house. Pass though these and climb to a telegraph pole where there is an old path which runs parallel to the road. After about 800m, it descends by two more gates to a second house on the road. Walk west and uphill along the road for 500m to a gate marked for Urgha before a bridge. Pass through the gate and take the path ahead which leads delightfully back through Glen Laxadale and along the lochs to the Scalpay road. Follow the road to the start (6h).

◄ Sunset on Toddun from Reinigeadal

On the Toe Head machair

Chaipaval (368m)

Walk time **4h + detour 20 min**
Height gain **400m**
Distance **13km** OS Map **Landranger 18**

Short route across the rich machair and rough ground of an unusual peninsula to view the natural architecture of Toe Head, with a return overlooking the white sands of Scarista Beach.

Start at the MacGillivray Centre, 4km northwest of Leverburgh (GR988903). Walk north to the end of the road, and take the track beyond for 800m to a gate and crossroads. Choose the track at roughly two o'clock (north) which heads towards a neat band of pink crags on the hillside. This leads to a series of sheep pens, which can be avoided on the left side to reach a gate. Pass through the gate into open country. There is a choice of routes to the top of Chaipaval: bear directly northwest for the steepest approach over clumpy heather or traverse more easily northwards across two runnels and double back southwest over the grasses. Either approach takes you to the summit with trig point and cairn beyond (GR973924) (1h20). Bear northwest to a boggy bealach and climb to a second top. This provides a good view of nearby Taransay, and it is even possible to see St Kilda on a clear day. Descend northwest

along the prominent and meandering ridge towards Toe Head, and down to flatter ground. [Detour: visit the tip of Toe Head and its natural sea arch (add 20 min).] Walk east to the Geo na Gainmhich, which hides a dank, tunnel-like second arch. Work your way clockwise around the coast: the uneven and often quaggy ground continues until you come to the firmer Sgeir Leomadail. Reach a fence after another 1km: pass through a gate just 100m from the steep coastline. The walking is now much easier with fine views of the Leverburgh Hills. Keep at this level to pass through another gate and then a third gate by a track. Follow the dunes and rabbit warrens of Scarista along the coast, and ford a small burn to a fourth gate where a grassy track leads to the original intersection. From here, it is a short way back to the start (4h).

The machair

The machair is the extensive low-lying fertile plain that lines much of the west coast of Harris, as well as the Uists. It is considered the rarest European habitat and is formed by the southwest winds blowing sand into dunes and then onto the boggier grassland beyond. The sand has a very high shell content (80-90%) and can also be fertilised with seaweed to create a rich environment that supports many flowers, including orchids. It is an important land for crofting but suffers Atlantic-strength storms.

◄ The bog and machair of Chaipaval from the road to Leverburgh

Eaval's maze

Eaval (347m)

Walk time 5h40 Height gain 500m
Distance 17km OS Map Landranger 18
and 22

**Eaval sits at the heart of a landscape
more suited to boat than walking, with
countless lochans, much rough ground
and very few paths.**

Start from the Roadends Sculpture at the
end of the road (a continuation of the B894)
on Loch Euphort (GR891631). Take the track
towards the house of Clachan Burrival, and
pass through a gate on the right hand side
to continue eastwards by the shore path.
Cross the stepping stones over the outflow
of Loch Obisary (good point to view leaping

salmon at certain times of year). Bear
southeast with more difficulty and over
boggy ground towards Burrival to reach a
fence and wooden gate. Beyond the gate,
tackle the steep slopes directly to a gap on
the north side, then traverse to the south
side to climb the steep summit knoll.
Burrival gives fine views and can help you
plan your return through the watery maze.
Descend southeast, zigzagging between
diamond-shaped crags to reach flatter
ground. Then climb one small knoll before
trending down to the far eastern end of
Loch Obisary with its delightful sandy bay.
Now the climbing begins: the warped east
ridge of Eaval can be followed by
negotiating steep heather runnels and crags

to lead you finally to the summit with trig point and rough shelter (GR899605) (2h20). Walk to a secondary cairn 200m to the southwest and then turn southeast, descending gentle slopes. Lower down, you may find a cave carved into the pink rock before continuing through bracken to Loch a'Gheàdais, roughly hewn as a five-pointed star. Skirt around the loch on its southern side to reach the sea. Follow the coastline northwards, descending to small bays littered with colourful stones and interesting flotsam. Pass two smaller lochs to reach Loch an Tomain with a nearby sea arch that you can walk across. From this point, leave the coast to head northwest. Weave around two arms of the loch, and then bear west to ascend two small knolls. Turn Burrival on its western side to rejoin the fence and wooden gate. Retrace your steps to the sculpture (5h40).

That sinking feeling

From the top of Eaval, it would appear that the Outer Hebrides are sinking. In fact, the Western Isles – along with most of northern Scotland – are slowly rising due to isostatic rebound: during the last ice age the weight of the ice forced down the earth's crust and it has been gradually 'springing back' since.

◀ Looking northwest from Eaval

Uist wilderness

Beinn Mhór (620m), **Beinn Corodale** (527m), **Hecla (606m)**

Walk time 10h Height gain 1300m
Distance 26km OS Map Landranger 22

Demanding walk over difficult ground with exposed mountain ridges, coastline and bog. Multiple summits with plenty of ascent, requiring lots of stamina and good route-finding skills.

Start from the end of the B890 at Loch Sgioport (GR828386). Midway between the last house and the road cutting, a path leads southwards. Follow this easily over two bridges and around two bays, past an old cottage and up to a shieling. The easy walking ends here. Keep to the coastline as you navigate bog and dense undergrowth, before bearing southwards to gain the east end of Loch Bèin. Climb eastwards under the buttresses of Maol Martaig to a bealach, and then pass through a wild chasm to reach the shore. Follow the

coastline south: soon the rocks are easier to negotiate than the grass and you reach an old cottage and a track. Follow the track for just 50m before it veers off to the lighthouse. Instead, continue south over rough grass and past a shieling to a boggy bealach, before making for the white-roofed Usinish Bothy (2h40). Continue along the coast for another 2km over difficult and convoluted ground which passes the east ridge of Beinn Corodale. This involves some ascent but brings you down to some old ruins and walled caves at Uamh a'Phrionnsa. Contour around Cas fo Dheas and climb beside the rapids to reach the foot of Loch Hellisdale. Rise westwards to a notch on the right of an overhanging crag by Maoladh nam Feannag. Continue westwards along the wide grassy east ridge of Beinn Mhór. Higher up, the cliffs of the northern corrie drop away suddenly but the going is fairly easy to the first cairn and the summit beyond (GR808311) (5h20). The top

◄ Beinn Corodale from Howmore

sits on vertical cliffs and the ridge beyond is fairly exposed, so care is required. Follow the ridge NNW, where a path switches sides every 200m, until the terrain eases. Trend north and then take the NE ridge, twisting down through boulders and folds to Bealach Hellisdale, identifiable by its many fenceposts. Make a rising traverse east to avoid steep ground, and then work your way northwards. The summit of Beinn Corodale is set back and has its own vertical north-facing cliffs. To descend and avoid the crags, head east for 120m and stop just before a small rise. Descend on the north side, making a westward diagonal between the crags and a knoll to reach the lower grassy slopes. These are still steep but lead northwest to a bealach, a wild place of bog, slabs and perched blocks. Climb north up grassy slopes onto Hecla and turn east to reach the rocky, scree-laden summit (GR826345) (7h40). Descend northeast and ascend a small cairned knoll: this gives access to the fine curving ridge of Beinn Scalabhat. Follow this first east and then north, where the ground becomes rougher, to reach Beinn na h-Aire and two consecutive cairns. Descend

northwards from here, sometimes awkwardly, to a bealach shared with Maol Martaig, where there is evidence of a grassy track. Descend westwards and then north over flat swampy land until you can see Loch Bèin. It's difficult to descend here, so walk westwards above the loch before bearing northwest over rough ground to reach the coast. Return to the start (10h).

Hills of Lochboisdale

Beinn Ruigh Choinnich (280m),
Triuirebheinn (357m)

Walk time **3h40** Height gain **500m**
Distance **10km** OS Map **Landranger 31**

**Half-day walk over two low hills with
some steep sections. Good navigation
skills are useful on this off-path route.**

Start at the large grey building and sign
for Braelea House, 1.5km northwest of
Lochboisdale Pier (GR785201). (Parking on
the main road.) Walk 100m northeast along
the minor road towards Lasgair. Pass over
the cattle grid to reach the first bend in the
road by a lamppost. Rather than follow the
road as it curves to the right, take the short

track ahead that serves two houses. Watch
for a grassy track after 20m, which skirts
around the east side of the house on the
right. The track leads you alongside a field
and down to a wooden bridge after 500m.
Cross the bridge and bear eastwards,
following a small path and animal trails.
Then bear southeast over undulating
ground before the slopes of Beinn Ruigh
Choinnich steepen suddenly: tackle these
directly to reach the summit cairns.
Descend northwards to Bealach an Easain
and its rounded barrel-like crags. Climb
northwards through the awkward heather
and long grasses of Triuirebheinn. There is
one false top to confuse you before you

◀ Lobster pots of Lochboisdale

gain the summit (GR813213) (2h20). Descend to the northwest, a complex ridge drops in waves and entails some switching back and forth to gain the easiest line. A perched block after 1km marks the steepest point before a boulder-scattered bealach. Descend west from here to find a track that cuts through the heather towards the

distant Loch Coragrimsaig. A white pipe cuts south across the land. Follow this or a raised heathery track just to the west. Continue south, and ford the burns that try to lead you westwards, to reach some low concrete buildings near Loch nan Smalag. A good grassy track leads westwards back to the bridge. Retrace your steps to the start (3h40).

23

Approaching from the sea, with the Cuillin hills shrouded in mist, the Vikings gave this land the name Skuyö, the Misty Isle. Today, Skye's rugged coastline and high escarpments draw thousands of tourists and walkers who come for adventure as well as the memorable mountain views.

The Cuillin are featured later in this book: the routes here cover other fascinating areas of Skye, with one circuit on the neighbouring Isle of Raasay, a short ferry ride away.

This section contains four routes on the long escarpment of the Trotternish. These include short circuits through the fantastic rock formations of the Quiraing and The Old Man of Storr, as well as two longer routes that cover the central part of the peninsula. A short walk begins close to Portree and a more involved circuit climbs the legendary MacLeod's Tables in Duirinish, returning along the wild coastline. Another part-coastal walk on Raasay climbs Dùn Caan. The final route takes in the hills above Kylerhea with commanding views of the Kintail mountains.

24

Skye and Raasay

Secrets of the Quiraing

Meall na Suiramach (543m)

Walk time **2h** Height gain **300m**
Distance **5km** OS Map Explorer 408

A fantastic landscape of needles, spires and crazy towers create a compact route with little ascent or technical difficulty.

Start from the car park at the top of the pass between Staffin and Uig (GR440678). A well-trodden path leads northeast, hugging the hillside beneath the steep cliffs of Meall na Suiramach. After winding past a knoll after 1km, this path trends over scree between the rocky bastion of The Prison on the right and the tottering pinnacle of The Needle by the main cliff. The path passes close to the rock as it turns north into complex terrain with miniature glens and lochans hidden by rocky fins. Where the path forks, continue north rather than dropping east. Pass over a wall to enter an enchanted dell: a magical place with

hundreds of places to hide if you are so inclined. Soon the path climbs steeply to the left to breach the crags and reach the ridge above. Another good path above Fir Bhreugach climbs southwards in an exposed position above the main crags, and here it becomes clear how The Table got its name. Bear west to reach the summit of Meall na Suiramach and descend by any route southwest over the heathery slopes of Maoladh Mór back to the start (2h).

Geology of the Trotternish

The Trotternish escarpment is evidence of volcanic activity 65 million years ago, which created a vast lava plateau across North Skye. Some of these lava flows are 10-15m thick and one such flow measures over 2km in width – the largest in Britain. Glacial and natural erosion have created the present landscape. Landslides have contributed to the unusual scenery at the Quiraing and The Storr, since the lava flows sit on particularly weak sedimentary rocks. The Table is large enough to hold six regiments or 4000 head of cattle and locals have reputedly played shinty on the top.

▼ Dun Dubh by the Quiraing

Fairy Glen of Uig

Beinn Edra (611m)

Walk time **5h40** Height gain **700m**
Distance **17km** OS Map Landranger 23

Great ridge walk in the Trotternish with views of the Quiraing. Accessed by farm roads and some rough walking, with plenty of interesting geology.

   Start by the Post Office and shop in Uig (GR397639). Almost directly opposite, there is a road marked for Glen Conon. Follow this east as it gains height in switchbacks. After 2km, the road ends at a farm. (No parking here.) Continue east through a series of sheep gates and take the grassy track beyond. This follows a slight incline and provides good walking, although the burn from Bealach nan Coisichean may be difficult to ford in spate. The track ends abruptly near old fencing: continue northeast over boggy ground to reach Bealach Uige. At this point, the steep escarpment of the Trotternish boasts a rock needle and superb views of the Quiraing. Climb SSE along the ridge as it rises and falls to reach the summit of Beinn Edra, its trig point set above steep cliffs (GR455627) (3h). Descend SSW along the ridge to Bealach a'Mhóramhain. Climb a small knoll, drop to Bealach Amadal and then ascend the slopes of Groba nan Each. Drop gently down the broad west ridge, which undulates

over Beinn an Laoigh before making another gradual descent. Beinn Fhuar is a classic moorland mound with hags and groughs: rather than get too involved with these, begin to drop gently northwest off the ridge. Any steep parts are short-lived and the descent brings you to an unusual raised ramp, running parallel to and some distance above the Lòn an t-Sratha. Follow the ramp northwest to soon reach some fenceposts to the right: accompany these down to a burn and then up for 80m where you will find an iron gate. Pass through the gate to enter a rough landscape of bog. This soon brings you to a track that leads through farm gates to Balnaknock and a minor road. Take the road as it meanders through the unusual grassy cones of Fairy Glen and back into Uig (5h40).

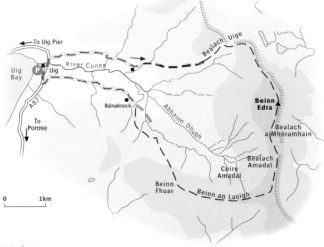

Mountain brew

The Isle of Skye Brewery (Leann an Eilean) in Uig was established in 1995 by two school teachers from Portree High. Today, the beer wins awards, and varieties include the slightly nutty Red Cuillin (4.2%), the dark and strong Black Cuillin (4.5%) and the full-bodied and refreshing Blaven (5%). Thirsty walkers are welcome to visit the brewery shop.

◀ Uig town and harbour

On the Trotternish

Hartaval (668m)

Walk time **7h** Height gain **900m**
Distance **18km** OS Map Landranger 23

A walk along the magnificent cliffs of the Trotternish, with steep sections, bog and a short stretch of road to return. Good navigation skills are essential.

Start at a large layby on the A855 directly opposite the turn-off for Lealt (GR516605). Walk west along the minor road to Lealt and continue by the track beyond. After around 2km, where the Lealt River changes course, the track leaves the water. Watch for the dismantled railway, now identifiable only by its raised profile, and follow this

instead, keeping dry above the clag. After 500m, leave the tracks and climb over undulating ground, veering west of Loch Liuravay and north of the craggy nose of the ridge to reach a flatter area with fenceposts below the east face of Sgùrr a'Mhadaidh Ruaidh. Climb south to gain the main west ridge. This leads easily to steeper ground: three shattered bands of cliffs can be breached on the south side of the face to reach the summit of Sgùrr a'Mhadaidh Ruaidh (GR474584) (2h40). Care should be taken as there are steep cliffs, especially on the north face, split by a gulch. Descend southwest to join the main Trotternish escarpment before climbing to the summit and tottering crags of Baca Ruadh. Continue south and drop awkwardly over scree to a bealach before Hartaval: it is another steep

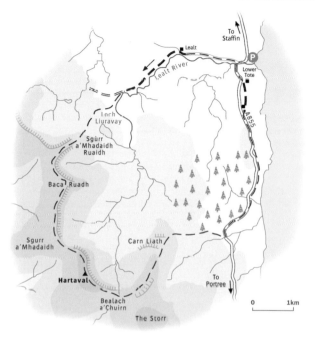

climb to the summit (GR480551) (4h). Descend by the southeast ridge to Bealach a'Chuirn. From this point ascend diagonally northeast to gain about 50m height, enough to keep above the parallel rock bands of The Storr's north ridge. Descend this with interest: after about 800m there is a sharp descent to the prominent rocky castle of Carn Liath before the ridge is scattered into boulders. Keep to the east side of this outcrop and drop east over grassy slopes, aiming for the corner of the forest. A fence can be followed part of the

way and then crossed by a stile near the trees. The forest has no good tracks close to the perimeter fence, so cross the bog directly east to reach the road after 500m. Walk northwards along the road for about 1km to the top of the hill. Here, you can join the old road which has a better view of the sea. This continues for 2km before merging with the new road again. Follow this for about 500m before turning right into Lower Tote, passing a house with a red roof: this road ends at the Lealt River close to the start (7h).

◄ Cliffs of Baca Ruadh

31

The Old Man of Storr

The Storr (719m)

Walk time **4h** Height gain **600m**
Distance **9km** OS Map **Explorer 408**

A compact route on a famous landmark, following good paths with several steep sections in ascent and descent.

Start at the car park and information panel by a large plantation on the A855 (GR507528). Take the marked path which climbs gracefully northwest through the forest, reaching a stile at the end of the trees. Cross the stile and continue along the main path towards the imposing cliffs of The Storr. The Old Man of Storr and his many smaller towers are indistinct at first but take shape as you gain height. Climb to the Sanctuary below the Old Man, a good place for a spot of exploring. Take another path which trends north to reach a gap between the main cliffs and a subsidiary knoll. Pass over a wall by a stile and continue around the rocky spur before a short step to the easier terrain of Coire Scamadal. Contour around the wide corrie to reach the north ridge of The Storr at a

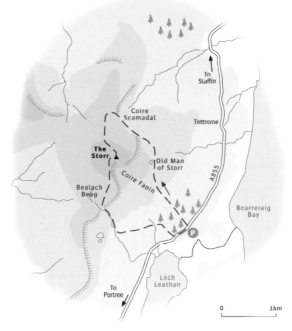

rocky tor. Turn south here, and begin the gentle climb to the summit and trig point (GR495541) (2h20). Descend with care as there are two notches with vertical cliffs, high above Coire Faoin. To avoid these safely, descend west for 200m from the summit before taking an easier line southwards, passing over small terraces to reach Bealach Beag at a cairn. A burn cascades steeply on the eastern side. Take the small path which accompanies the water on its left, with one steep section, to reach the lower grassy slopes. Descend over this gentler ground and past the plantation to reach a stile and the road. Retrace your steps to the start (4h).

Turned to stone

According to local legend, an old man and his wife lost one of their cows and, whilst out searching, met with some giants. They fled but made the mistake of looking back, and were turned to stone. The old man is still there, but his wife fell over many years ago.

◄ The Old Man of Storr with the Cuillin beyond

33

MacLeod's mountain feast

Healabhal Mhór (469m),
Healabhal Bheag (489m)

Walk time 9h Height gain 1000m
Distance 26km OS Map Landranger 23

**A great circuit that starts near Dunvegan
and crosses a varied landscape. The
return is long with a magnificent walk
across the clifftops, but this route is
escapable after the Tables.**

Start at a gate and track on the B884
between Dunvegan and Colbost
(GR243463). Take the muddy track south to
the ruins of Osdale, and then follow the
fenceline until close to the burn. Follow
the water upstream on its north bank for about
500m before crossing the burn at flatter
ground. Begin to climb westwards: low
crags and terraces make for an entertaining
ascent. The terrain rises steeply before
reaching the broad summit plateau of
Healabhal Mhór. Descend easily from the
southwest end over grassy slopes to the
boggy bealach of An Sgùrran. Start to climb
southwards but, rather than ascend the
knoll, make an easy traverse on the corrie
side to reach the northern slopes of
Healabhal Bheag. [Escape: take the east
ridge and descend to Orbost.] Walk around
to the east side to avoid scree slopes and
tackle the slopes to the summit
(GR224423) (3h). Descend the south ridge
directly: although steep, there are no
difficult sections. Pass over Bealach
Bharcasaig and cross to the Ollisdal Lochs.
Descend south to follow a small burn. As it
enters Coire Mór, the water drops steeply:
you can avoid an awkward descent by
taking easier slopes to the left before
rejoining the burn. Cross and keep to the
west side down to the bothy in Glen
Ollisdal. Cross the burn and descend
towards the coast to follow the spectacular
clifftops southeast. A 1km walk takes you to

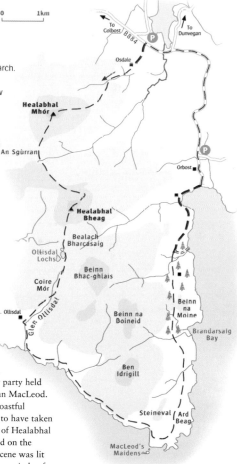

◄ Cliffs of Duirinish near Glen Ollisdal

sea stacks colonised by birds, a dramatic waterfall and a rocky arch. Continue by the coastal path to MacLeod's Maidens. Then follow the path as it turns northwards between Steineval and Ard Beag to descend to a fence and new plantation. The path climbs over a ridge and above Brandarsaig Bay to enter Rebel's Wood, planted in memory of punk legend Joe Strummer. Continue over Beinn na Moine and down to join a forest track. Turn left to follow the track through newly harvested trees. Later, where it reaches a gate and cottage, the track improves. Follow it towards Orbost and then north for 4km along minor roads to the start or Dunvegan (9h).

MacLeod's Tables

The popular name for the flat-topped hills near Dunvegan derives from a legendary dinner party held by the 16th-century chief of Clan MacLeod. Returning the hospitality of a boastful southern lord, MacLeod is said to have taken his guest at dusk to the summit of Healabhal Mhór. A feast had been prepared on the mountaintop and the amazing scene was lit by the chief's 'candlesticks', a huge circle of torch-bearing clansmen.

35

Ben Tianavaig by Portree

Tianavaig (413m)

Walk time **2h40** Height gain **400m**
Distance **8km** OS Map Landranger 23

A gentle hill with fine geology and some rough ground to start and finish. This makes a good wet weather alternative to some of the longer routes. Dogs are not allowed on this hill.

Start from the two picnic benches by Tianavaig Bay in Camastianavaig (GR508389). (Limited parking here.) Walk north along the road for 50m and cross the bridge. Turn right immediately after the bridge to take a grassy path between the burn and a fence to the shore. Follow the shoreline eastwards, taking a rough route by a fence through trees or along the pebbles when the tide is low. After passing an old half-hidden wall, start to climb gently – still keeping to the coast. When you have a clear view of the sea, the path splits: descend slightly to pass along an interesting ledge beneath a crag. Then continue along the coast at this level – roughly 10-20m above the sea – until you reach a level grassy promontory. Cross this and continue to follow the coastline beneath more cliffs until you are almost level with two square blocks about 30m offshore. Leave the coast here to climb steep grassy slopes westwards to a flat scree-covered area. Beyond the scree, aim for the hypnotic diamond-shaped shield, passing the tranquil McQueen's Loch and ascending steep heather and grass to reach it. Now turn northwest over easier ground to reach the main ridge. A short walk south leads to the summit of Ben Tianavaig (GR512410) (2h). Follow vague paths along the exposed south ridge, with great views to sea. On approaching Camastianavaig, head towards the two easternmost houses over complex and difficult ground. Just above these houses and their gardens, there is a large rowan tree. A hidden path lies to the right of the tree and leads between the two gardens. Follow the path down to the road and the start point (2h40).

Battle of the Braes

The district of Braes, from Tianavaig Bay down to Loch Sligachan, was the scene in 1882 for what was, arguably, the last battle on British soil. Refused grazing rights on Ben Lee and threatened with eviction, crofters fought with police who came from Inverness to arrest them. Warships and marines were dispatched by the alarmed authorities, but the dispute soon fizzled out and the Napier Commission was set up shortly after to inquire into the crofters' grievances. This resulted in the Crofters Act of 1886, providing security of tenure.

◀ Portree harbour

Dùn Caan of Raasay

Dùn Caan (443m)

Walk time **5h40** Height gain **500m**
Distance **17km** OS Map **Landranger 24**

Raasay's iconic peak, reached through wood and over moorland with a return by a deserted village and along the shore. This route contains a steep but avoidable descent.

Start at Raasay Pier (GR554342). Head north along the road towards Inverarish and, about 50m west of the pier, cross a fence by a gate to gain access to the old mine railway. Climb the steep grassy embankment and follow the remains of the mine railway past odd buildings. Pass through a cutting, over a stile and northwards across the moor, following the elevated route of the railway. After about 1km, you will come to a building and the start of a plantation. Cross a fence by a stile and follow the forest break to join green path markers after 200m: these lead you on a northerly descent into a ravine to reach a single-track road by derelict buildings. Continue straight on over a bridge to follow Burma Road for about 500m. Just after crossing another bridge, take the path signposted for Dùn Caan. This path (with occasional bog) shadows Inverarish Burn. After 2.5km, at a cairn, the terrain levels out and gives a full view of the mountain.

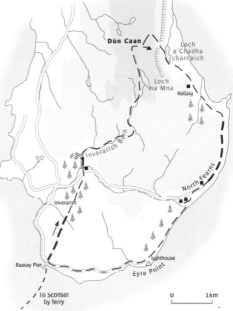

Just beyond is a fence with a stile. Cross this and head across moorland to Loch na Mna, which is easily passed on the west. Bear north across slopes to pick up the steep profile of Dùn Caan: a zigzag path takes you to the summit (GR579395) (2h40). Descend the way you came for a short while, and then head north to flatter ground. Begin to drop southeast, bearing in mind there are steep cliffs beyond. Aim for the mid-point of Loch a'Chadha chàrnaich to find a large rock prow which juts from the cliffs. It is easy to scramble down between the fin and the main escarpment and, from here, steep grass slopes lead down to the loch. Cross a fence and keep to the loch with its wooded islands before heading southeast over boggy ground to the deserted township of Hallaig. [Variant: for an easier descent, keep above all cliffs for about 1km until they peter out and then bear east to reach Hallaig.] From the most southerly ruin, descend southeast to a ravine. Cross the burn and join a path which rises slightly before contouring across open ground, into birch and past a cairn. Further south, this becomes a grassy track that takes you to North Fearns and a road. Just before the second house (this is the first house on the left), turn off the road to take a path down to the coast. When below the third house, turn directly to the shore to reach a tiny boathouse. Follow the coastline, either on the pebbly beach or by a path in the trees. Just before the lighthouse at Eyre Point, watch for a grassy track which leads you to the road. Follow this back to the pier (5h40).

◄ Raasay from The Storr

Crossing Kylerhea

Sgùrr na Coinnich (739m),
Ben Aslak (610m)

Walk time 6h Height gain 1100m
Distance 12km OS Map Landranger 33

**Compact off-path route that begins
with a steep climb and contains sections
of bog. Good navigation is required. In
summer, a ferry runs between Glenelg in
Kintail and Kylerhea.**

Start in Kylerhea at the car park and start
of the track to the Kylerhea Otter Haven
(GR786211). Immediately, begin the steep
climb northwest over springy heather.
Higher up, the angle relents and the
undergrowth is less pervasive and scattered

with slabs, leading you to two cairns at the
top of Beinn Bhuidhe. Follow the quaggy
ground towards the east ridge of Sgùrr na
Coinnich and then climb the spur, passing
veins of quartz, to reach the summit
(GR762222) (2h20). Walk southwest, losing
height in fits and starts to reach a lochan
after 400m. Now descend southwards along
the south ridge with its views into Coire na
Coinnich. Where the ridge begins to
contort, descend southwest to join a burn.
This can be followed with ease past a
waterfall and down to lower ground which
leads you to the road at its highest point,
Bealach Udal. Cross the road and follow a
short track past a green building to a mast.

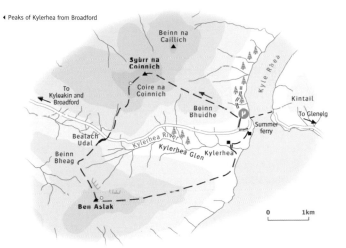

◄ Peaks of Kylerhea from Broadford

Climb southwest over tussocky grass (this makes for tough walking). Higher up, several knolls pretend to be the top of Beinn Bheag: ignore them and instead turn south to a steep dip leading to the northwest slopes of Ben Aslak. Climb firmer ground, passing low crags to reach the convoluted top. The highest point is just to the southwest of a summit lochan (GR750191) (4h20). From the lochan, bear east past several cairns to follow the fine east ridge: it is best to keep quite close to the edge above Kylerhea Glen rather than let slopes trick you southwards. Further down, there is boggy ground before a prominent knoll: keep to the left of this and continue your bearing, descending more steeply to join a path close to the sea. Follow the path northwards, keeping by an old fence to pass some ruins. When the fence approaches the river, look for a footbridge just to the left. Cross the bridge and follow the path to a road. Follow this easily back to the start (6h).

Swimming cows

In 1773, when Johnson and Boswell left Glenelg to continue their famous tour, this was the main ferry route from Skye to the mainland. It was also the way across for drovers and their cattle. The beast were tied with ropes from horn to tail and the leading animal was held by the horns by one drover in the stern of the boat, while another rowed the boat across.

The Red Cuillin are rounded, scree-covered domes that make for great half-day routes, give fantastic views and will often bask in the sun when higher peaks are in mist. The Black Cuillin are another matter. They are the Scottish Alps, once a training ground for Himalayan mountaineers. The terrain is complex: there are too many crags to be marked on any map and compasses are unreliable due to the gabbro rock. Ridges become knife-edged and then end in cliffs without warning and, while rock quality is mostly good, many parts have loose and tottering blocks. Vast tumbling scree fields guard the flanks, long sections of the main ridge are inescapable, there are few places for shelter and the peaks are often bathed in thick mist.

The routes here are not definitive. It is advisable to thoroughly research any intended route with other sources, particularly the descents and escapes. Scrambling and climbing skills as well as ropecraft are prerequisites. You will also need stamina and concentration as well as excellent navigation skills and a good sense of mountain awareness. However, there is no substitute for local knowledge and many choose to hire a guide. This is strongly recommended.

The Cuillin of Skye

The Bloody Stone

Sgùrr nan Gillean ⓜ (965m)

Walk time **8h** Height gain **1000m**
Distance **19km**
Harvey Map **Skye: The Cuillin**

Long approach through a dramatic corrie to reach one of the Cuillin's best-known peaks, with exposure, scrambling and complex navigation. Good paths but some rougher terrain in access.

Start at the Sligachan Hotel (GR485298). Cross the old bridge to the east bank of the River Sligachan and immediately take a path on the right signposted for Loch Coruisk. This path leads southwards through Glen Sligachan: follow it easily for about 5.5km until the River Sligachan flows from the west. Leave the path here, and trend southwestwards across the boggy watershed. At times of severe flood, the glen may not be passable but this is rare. Keep close to the south bank as you pass the Bloody Stone and follow vague tracks into the Harta Corrie. Cross the water below the cascades from the hanging Lota Corrie. Climb steeply east between the rocky peak of Sgùrr na h-Uamha and Sgùrr Beag over slabs and scree to reach a bealach on the southeast ridge of Sgùrr nan Gillean. The summit of Sgùrr Beag can be climbed or turned on the west flank. Traverse the arête northwest, on the crest or on either Lota Corrie. About 500m on from Sgùrr Beag, the ridge begins to climb: this point marks the descent so is worth noting. Climb the ridge directly: this involves some scrambling,

The Bloody Stone

The huge boulder known as the Bloody Stone was the site of an atrocious clan massacre in 1601. Driven to a defensive position there by MacDonalds, a party of MacLeods were slaughtered and their bodies piled around the rock. Legend has it that their bones became bows and arrows for the local fairies.

with increasing exposure, and any ascent must be down-climbed afterwards. The easiest lines are on the south side of the crest: the north side is loose and the scene of many bad accidents. Surmount slabs, blocks and short walls to reach the airy summit: space for a small party only (GR472253) (5h20). Retrace your steps to the start of the climbing on the ridge. Descend on the east flank, losing height on a diagonal route across an open bowl of scree (occasional cairns). The northern boundary of this face has a steep band of crags overlooking scree slopes (above) and enclosed corrie with waterfalls (below). Break through the band of rock on an easy but exposed leftwards descent marked with cairns. This leads to the scree slopes: follow these down to easier ground. A path takes you northwards from here under the steep buttresses of Pinnacle Ridge. After about 600m, this drops steeply into Coire Riabhach. Skirt around this corrie and climb slightly to join a purpose-built path. Follow this northwards to reach a bridge over the Allt Dearg Beag. On the other side, the path follows the burn downstream for a short distance and then crosses the moor. Another bridge, this time over the Allt Dearg Mór, brings you within a few minutes' walk of the Sligachan Hotel (8h).

◀ Pinnacle Ridge on Sgùrr nan Gillean

45

The Executioner

Am Basteir ⓜ (935m),
Bruach na Frithe ⓜ (958m)

Walk time **6h + detour 1h**
Height gain **1000m** Distance **13km**
Harvey Map **Skye: The Cuillin**

A challenging route with some complex navigation over a mixture of scree and rock – and an optional scramble to gain The Executioner.

Start at the Sligachan Hotel (GR485298). Walk along the Carbost road for about 300m until just past the mountain rescue centre. Look for a path on the left, which leads south to a bridge across the Allt Dearg Mór. Cross the bridge, and continue south over moorland on an excellent path to reach the Allt Dearg Beag. Follow this burn upstream for 1.5km. Before reaching the spectacular Bhasteir Gorge, climb southwest over scree and around short crags to the top of Meall Odhar, a fine hill with the best view across to Pinnacle Ridge. Turn south to cross the rounded bealach and climb the fun northwest ridge of Sgùrr a'Bhasteir. The arête has many low crags that can be turned or scrambled as desired to reach the top (GR464257) (2h40). Continue along a level rocky ridge to Bealach nan Lice. [Detour: to ascend Am Basteir (The Executioner), descend northeast into Coire a'Bhasteir, following a path over the scree. Then take a steep scree chute to join the main ridge between Sgùrr nan Gillean and the north-facing cliffs of Am Basteir. Bear west along the exposed arête:

46

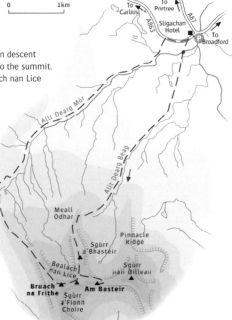

◄ The Executioner's Tooth

there is one very tricky move in descent before easy scrambling leads to the summit. Return the same way to Bealach nan Lice (add 1h)]. Climb south from Bealach nan Lice, keeping right of a tower just west of the Bhasteir Tooth. On the other side of the tower, a gap looks down into Harta Corrie and provides climbing access to the Tooth (for rock-climbers only). Climb west under the flanks of Sgùrr a'Fionn Choire (or climb this subsidiary by an easy detour), and continue easily to the summit of Bruach na Frithe (4h) (GR461252). Descend by the defined northwest ridge: a path keeps to the left of the spur and allows for easy progress. Lower down the ridge loses definition; keep your bearing to reach Bealach a'Mhaim. Pick up an excellent path on the far side of the boggy ground and

small lochans. Follow the path northeast along the Allt Dearg Mór and back to Sligachan (6h).

Climbing on Skye

The period from the 1880s to the outbreak of the Great War was a golden age in Scottish mountaineering, and saw early and steep climbs on Ben Nevis and the Cuillin. The publication of OS maps in the 1880s, the railways and then the arrival of the motor car all helped to develop mountaineering. The pioneers included Harold Raeburn, Norman Collie and William Naismith, whose climbs are still celebrated today. Equipment was basic, with tweeds the only waterproofing. Ropes would break easily, and all climbers respected the rule that the leader should never fall.

Three from Glen Brittle

Sgùrr a'Mhadaidh ⓜ(918m),
Sgùrr a'Ghreadaidh ⓜ(973m),
Sgùrr na Banachdich ⓜ (965m)

Walk time **6h** Height gain **1300m**
Distance **10km**
Harvey Map **Skye: The Cuillin**

A compact but exciting route with lots of ascent and several points of exposed scrambling and easy climbing. Consider taking a rope for harder sections.

Start from the youth hostel in Glen Brittle (GR409225). Take a good path immediately opposite the hostel to follow the south bank of the Allt a'Choire Ghreadaidh. The route steepens gradually to take you into Coire a'Ghreadaidh after 2.5km. Thereafter, climb northeast into Coire An Dorus keeping close to the burn.

Weave carefully over scree-covered rocks to the obvious bealach between Sgùrr Thuilm and Sgùrr a'Mhadaidh. Scramble up the rocky and intimidating west ridge of Sgùrr a'Mhadaidh. This involves some entertaining moves through corners and over slabs: keeping to the right (south side) reduces both difficulty and exposure. Higher up, the ascent eases and leads to the summit (3h) (GR447235). Descend southwards from the top, keeping to the

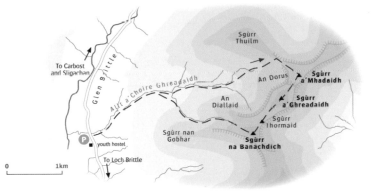

Glen Brittle side until close to An Dorus: a steep-sided bealach. The hardest part is the final few metres into the gulch, with a short slippery scramble. [Escape: descend west into Coire An Dorus.] From the gash, a tricky rock step of climbing that starts on the Glen Brittle side provides the technical crux of the route. This leads to easier but exposed terrain above: keep to the east side of the ridge to pass the gap of Eag Dubh before scrambling up to join the apex. Beyond lies The Wart, a long buttress of dark overhanging gabbro. Pass The Wart on the west side to reach the knife-edge summit of Sgùrr a'Ghreadaidh. The short traverse to the south top is wildly exposed. Descend the southwest ridge with interest, turning any difficulties on the west, to

reach the Thormaid Ghreadaidh gap. Climb south to pass three teeth on the east side by a narrow ledge (they can also be scrambled directly), then ascend slabs to reach the summit of Sgùrr Thormaid. From the top, drop a little to the west side over awkward broken rock for 15m and traverse easily to rejoin the ridge. Descend this more easily over broken rock to Bealach Thormaid. The ascent to the summit of Sgùrr na Banachdich is straightforward. Leave by the west ridge and watch for a subsidiary spur bearing northwest. This leads to Coire an Eich. Drop easily to the west over scree to reach easier grassy terrain. Strike northwest to join the original path along the Allt a'Choire Ghreadaidh which leads back to the hostel (6h).

Marking the boundaries

Sgùrr a'Ghreadaidh translates in Gaelic as 'Peak of the Thrashing' which may relate to the clan tradition of beating young boys at the boundaries of territory so that they would always remember where the markers were. Alternatively it might refer to the mighty winds which buffet the peak.

◄ Looking north along the Cuillin Ridge from Sgùrr Alasdair

49

Alasdair and the In Pinn

Sgùrr Alasdair ⓜ (993m),
Sgùrr Mhic Coinnich ⓜ (948m),
Sgùrr Dearg (the **In Pinn**) ⓜ (986m)

Walk time 9h20 Height gain 1200m
Distance 11km
Harvey Map Skye: The Cuillin

Long route over multiple tops with plenty of ascent, continual exposure and complex navigation around towers and buttresses. An abseil descent from the In Pinn is recommended: a rope is also useful on other tricky sections.

Start from Glen Brittle by the campsite at the end of the road (GR409205). Take the track through the campsite, and cross a stile behind the toilet block. Follow the path beyond and turn left at the first fork towards Coire Lagan. Shortly after passing Loch an Fhir-bhallaich, watch for a narrow path on the right. Take this path to traverse the corrie floor and climb to the base of Sròn na Ciche and the hanging Cioch. Make your way eastwards under the cliffs, climbing over scree. This leads to the Sgumain Stone Chute, a gully choked with the debris of a very large and recent rockfall. The large boulders at the centre of the chute make for an entertaining ascent to Bealach Coir'a Ghrunnda. Climb easily northwards to reach the summit of Sgùrr Sgumain (3h). The rest of the route involves great exposure and technical difficulty. [Escape: return to Bealach Coir'a Ghrunnda and reverse the route or descend by Coire a'Ghrunnda (harder).] Walk to a gap just to the south of the top, and descend on the north side over slabs for 20m. An easy traverse leads to a series of pinnacles. Descend on the south side by a short corner (large cave). Traverse under the pinnacles to reach the steep walls of Sgùrr Alasdair.

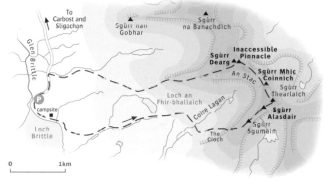

About 30m south (right) of the ridge, there is a short corner that involves easy rock-climbing. Beyond, easy scrambling leads to the exposed top of Skye's highest peak: its views are intimidating in any weather (GR450208). Descend to the east, scrambling past steep drops to the head of the Great Stone Chute. Descend on the south (right) side for about 50m over the scree beneath the rocky snout of Sgùrr Thearlaich's south ridge. Look for an easy point to breach the buttress and then climb NNW to the top. Walk along the fine crest: after about 150m, this reaches a gap before a stumpy tower and the start of steep ground with many options. A descent on the right (east) is recommended as the easiest to follow. Take a diagonal line over slabs with two short sections of down-climbing: it is then possible to traverse into Bealach Mhic Coinnich. Climb up blocky steps and follow Collie's Ledge on the Coire Lagan side, rejoining the ridge after about 100m. [Detour: Sgùrr Mhic Coinnich is reached more easily from the north side and involves some more scrambling.] From this

point, the ridge eases for a short time to reach Bealach Coire Lagan. An Stac provides great scrambling and easy rock-climbing. To start, climb a loose fin just to the left of the apex of the ridge. About 50m up, hug the arête for inescapable climbing on mostly good holds. Cross a hanging slab on the east side of the top and bridge a gap to reach the bottom of the In Pinn. Most teams will rope up for the In Pinn. The crux is just beyond a midway belay ledge. Descend by abseil on the north end. [Variant: climbing on An Stac can be avoided by taking a rake of scree on the Coire Lagan side to reach the In Pinn much higher up. The In Pinn can also be avoided easily on the south side.] The summit of Sgùrr Dearg is just beyond (GR444216) (8h). Descend southwest to take a fine ridge: this leads to a short section of easy scrambling over Sgùrr Dearg Beag. Descend west, dropping steeply over the final nose to gain a good path. This passes the splendid cascades of Eas Mór and leads down to Glen Brittle. A short walk along the glen takes you back to the start (9h20).

Wilds of Loch Coruisk

Gars-bheinn (895m), **Sgùrr nan Eag** ⓜ
(924m), **Sgùrr Dubh Mór** ⓜ (944m)

Walk time 7h + detour 1h Height gain
1100m Approach and return 5h walk
Distance 11km + 14km approach and
return Harvey Map Skye: The Cuillin

**Complex navigation, scrambling,
optional rock-climbing, multiple river
crossings and a long approach mean this
is a route for the real adventurer.
Check tide times and complete after
dry weather, or consider taking the**
Bella Jane **from Elgol.**

Start from a parking area on the B8083,
5km north of Elgol and just south of
Kirkibost (GR545173). Pass through a gate
and take the track westwards, heading for
Camasunary. The track climbs over the brow
of the hill and zigzags down to the house
and bothy on the sandy flatlands of
Camasunary. The river beyond can be hard
to cross and the lower part is tidal: walk

upstream for about 400m to find stepping
stones over the water. On the far bank, walk
southwards to pick up broken paths around
the headland. This circumnavigates Sgùrr na
Stri and can be hard going: the best line
keeps about 30m above the sea. The Bad
Step is encountered on reaching Loch na
Leachd: a set of steep slabs that drop
straight into the water. The easiest traverse
line involves keeping low past the cave and
following an easy crack, but the difficulties
can be avoided by climbing about 40m in
height to the right of the slabs and
descending diagonally above them all.
Cross the boulderfield around the bay and
follow the path to the stepping stones. Ford
the foot of Loch Coruisk and bear west to
pass close to the locked JMCS Coruisk Hut.
[Variant: this point can be reached by boat
from Elgol.] Walk times start from here.
Follow the coast around Loch na Cuilce
(difficult at high tide) to the Mad Burn. Take
a rising path which follows the coastline:

52

◄ The Cuillin from Elgol

this passes a set of blocky south-facing crags and then reaches a deep bowl just beyond Eilean Reamhar. At this point, start to climb southwest up steep slopes of scree and heather to reach the defined east ridge of Gars-bheinn. This leads easily over the top of exposed cliffs to the summit (GR468187) (2h20). Descend slightly west from the summit to avoid a steep gap and then follow the main ridge north, to easily reach Sgùrr a'Choire Bhig after a short climb. Descend northwest from here over rocky terraces to a prominent bealach. Sgùrr nan Eag looms ahead with wild gabbro cliffs on its eastern aspect. An entertaining ascent leads up through boulders and runnels to reach the long and rocky summit. Descend the north ridge: this provides some scrambling, with complex route-finding, mostly taken on the west side of the apex to reach Bealach a'Garbh-choire. [Escape: descend to the east below Caisteal a'Garbh-choire to Loch Coruisk, keeping close to the side of Sgùrr Dubh Mór.] Caisteal a'Garbh-choire can be avoided by traversing on the east side or can be taken

directly (rock-climbing from the south followed by an abseil or down-climb on the west) to reach the north side of the 'castle'. Climb through high boulders to the top of Sgùrr Dubh an Da Bheinn (5h). [Detour: descend along the east arête to a bealach. Sgùrr Dubh Mór is a tricky scramble and it is best to keep on the south side up corners and over pinnacles to an exposed summit. Return to the main ridge (add 1h).] Descend easily northwest to Bealach Coir'an Lochain. At the prominent gap on the ridge, drop to the east side and follow slabs and scree down to Coir'an Lochain. Accompany the exit burn on the right hand side for about 200m, and then follow a series of cairns in a diagonal descent between bands of slabs around a blunt ridge. Navigation is important here: this part keeps you separated from the steep crags of Sgùrr Dubh Mór by one band of slabs. This leads more easily into Coir a'Chaoruinn where burns can be followed with few difficulties to the head of Loch Coruisk. Walk southeast along the shore to the foot of the loch (7h). Retrace your steps back to civilisation.

53

Blaven

Clach Glas (786m), **Blà Bheinn** ⓜ(928m)

Walk time **6h40** Height gain **1100m**
Distance **10km**
Harvey Map **Skye: The Cuillin**

When seen across Loch Slapin in the early morning, Blà Bheinn is a strong contender for Scotland's most beautiful peak. This route involves considerable exposure, scrambling and a difficult descent. A rope is recommended.

Start above the shores of Loch Slapin where the Allt na Dunaiche flows along the north of a large plantation (GR561217). (There is a large car park here.) Follow the path close to the north bank of the burn.

Rather than cross the main flow, follow the northern tributary into the flats of Choire a'Caise. Climb steadily over the grass and scree of the corrie, keeping to the gentler southern side beneath the imposing buttresses of Clach Glas. Higher up, the scree makes progress more difficult and culminates in a bealach on the main ridge south of Sgùrr nan Each. Climb south along the ridge: this is complex and requires deviations on the right hand side around pinnacles. Avoid the last pinnacle on the right to reach a scree gully below a large tower. Climb to the top of this and look for a water-worn chimney on the Glen Sligachan side. This gives pleasant rock-

climbing with a few tricky moves to start but becomes easier with good holds to reach the summit ridge. Easy scrambling on slabs lead to the top of Clach Glas, known as the Matterhorn of Skye (GR533222) (3h). Descend via the exposed and difficult south ridge, at first leftwards over a slab known as The Imposter. This ends in a small overhang giving access to the crest. Follow this until it drops suddenly, then turn all of the main difficulties below on the Slapin (left) side of the arête: an exposed and technical descent. This gains easier ground and a gap on the ridge. Climb steeply out of this and pass a tower on the left to reach the Putting Green, a fine picnic spot with the best views of The Great Prow. Continue into the confusing array of towers on Blà Bheinn's north face: gain a small dip and climb a short rock face to gain a boulderfield. This is easily followed right to reach a large scree gully trending to the left. This finishes in an intimidating right-facing chimney: fine rock climbed on good

holds leads to the main ridge above. The main summit of Blà Bheinn is an easy walk from here (GR530217) (5h). Make one final scramble to gain the south top which offers magnificent views down to Loch Coruisk. Descend with ease via the southeast flank. This reaches a gap before an outlying knoll at the head of Coire Uaigneich. Drop northeast through the boulder-strewn glen on a good path. Lower down, the path crosses the Allt na Dunaiche to return to the start (6h40).

Gaelic alphabet

Blaven's Gaelic name is Blà Bheinn (mountain of bloom), with the *bh* representing the letter *v* which is not present in the 18-letter Gaelic alphabet (j,k,q,w,x,y and z are not used either). Skye's Gaelic College, Sabhal Mòr Ostaig, on the Sleat peninsula, offers courses for beginners in the language – as well as having the only Gaelic-speaking elevator in the world.

◀ Blà Bheinn and Loch Slapin from Torrin

Into the Red Cuillin

Beinn na Cro (572m)

Walk time **4h** Height gain **600m**
Distance **10km**
Harvey Map **Skye: The Cuillin**

A low peak of the Red Cuillin with great views of Blà Bheinn. Good access paths and no route-finding difficulties or scrambling on this walk.

Start at the Am Bothan tearoom and shop in Torrin (GR575200). (Park north of the village on the B8083 to Elgol.) Directly opposite the shop is a driveway to two houses. Follow this north until it bends to

the right and then leave the drive to continue north over rough ground, keeping a fence on your right. Soon, you can pick up a good path that crosses a burn and continues north. The path then follows Srath Beag, keeping height above the river, to reach the bealach before An Slugan after about 3km. Leave the path near the bealach, and bear northwest over grassland and the awkward heather of Gualann nam Fiadh to reach the north ridge of Beinn na Cro. Follow the ridge southwards: the rocky upper slopes provide easier walking before steepening towards a sheltered stone circle

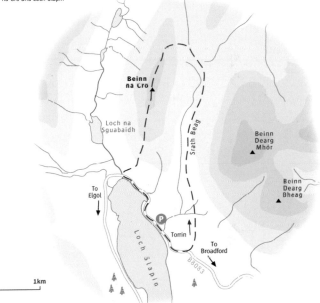

◀ Beinn na Cro and Loch Slapin

and the summit (GR569242) (2h40). Descend directly by the south ridge. After about 500m there is a subtle split in the spur to accommodate a burn: keep to the west side to lose height quickly. Lower down, the slopes become boggy but soon lead down to the road by a bridge. Walk back along the shore to Torrin (4h).

The Cuillin of Skye

The Black and Red Cuillin are named according to the colour of the dominant rock type. The spectacular formations of the Black Cuillin are mostly comprised of Gabbro, an older rock. The Red Cuillin with their distinctive frost-shattered scree slopes are formed from granite. Both rock types were originally the magma chambers of the volcanoes that once dominated Western Scotland. These rocks have been extensively studied since the 1800s by well-known geologists such as Sir Archibald Geikie, Professor John Wesley Judd and Dr Alfred Harker.

Peaks of Broadford

Beinn Dearg Mhór (709m),
Beinn na Caillich (732m)

Walk time **4h20** Height gain **1000m**
Distance **10km**
Harvey Map **Skye: The Cuillin**

**Great ridge walk with easy access from
Broadford but some rough sections in
approach and return.**

Start from Old Corry at the end of the
public road (GR619227). (Limited parking.
This point can also be reached easily on
foot from Broadford via the Elgol road.)
Strike westwards across the moor, reaching
an old wall after 200m. Aim for the east
ridge of Beinn Dearg Bheag as you gain
height over the heather. Cross the Allt
Beinn Deirge and start to climb the ridge.
A good path winds its way up, passing over
one false top before reaching the summit
of Beinn Dearg Bheag. Descend the north
ridge on its west side to a bealach: this
can be awkward, with scree and boulders
which try to force you leftwards. Climb the
blunt nose of Beinn Dearg Mhór, with its
loose covering of scree and soil, to reach
the summit overlooking Blà Bheinn and
the Black Cuillin (GR588228) (2h40).

◄ Approaching Beinn Dearg Bheag

Drop easily ENE to a bealach before climbing to the top of Beinn na Caillich with its huge cairn: the northern corries are steep and care should be exercised here. There is a choice of ridges to descend. the least trodden is to descend north for about 200m before trending NNW along a prominent spur over grass and scree between Coire Reidh and Coire Seamraig. After losing considerable height, drop east off the ridge into the bowl. Traverse Coire Seamraig and cross under the northeast ridge, then descend southeast, crossing the Allt a'Choire. Follow vague tracks down to Old Corry and back to the start (4h20).

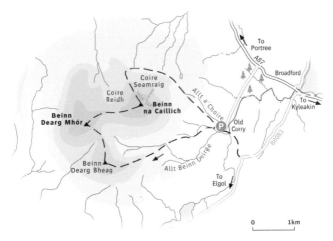

The Gift of the Prince

In 1746, Bonnie Prince Charlie was helped in his flight from Scotland by Captain John MacKinnon of Strathaird. In return the Prince gave MacKinnon the secret recipe of his personal liqueur, one of his few possessions. The drink, christened Drambuie (*An dram buidheach*: the drink that satisfies), was made by the MacKinnons on Skye for their own consumption for over a century before being sold to the public for the first time in the Broadford Inn in 1893. Today, 'The Gift of the Prince' is a global brand with the Drambuie company headquarters in Edinburgh.

Horseshoe on the Red Cuillin

Glamaig ⒢ (775m),
Beinn Dearg Mhór (731m)

Walk time **5h** Height gain **1300m**
Distance **11km**
Harvey Map Skye: The Cuillin

**The outlook from these hills is often
clear when the Black Cuillin are
engulfed in mist. This route contains
steep ascent and descent over scree and
some rough ground in approach.**

  Start from the Sligachan Hotel
(GR485298). Cross to the east bank of the
River Sligachan by the old bridge and
immediately take a path on the right,
signposted for Loch Coruisk, to bear
southwards along Glen Sligachan. After

about 300m, leave the main path and pass
though a stile on the left to follow the Allt
Daraich as it twists through a leafy ravine.
After about 400m, you will reach a gate in a
fence close to the river. Pass through the
gate and seek to cross the burn: it is usually
easy to jump but there are also metal rungs
to help you. On the far side, bear northeast
over boggy and bumpy ground towards the
imposing mass of Glamaig. Then begin the
hard climb up the slopes: this is never too
steep, and grass runnels and paths wind
through the rocks most of the way. Higher
up, the terrain eases for a while above a
vague northern corrie; thereafter, scree
leads to the summit of Glamaig (GR513300)
(2h20). Walk eastwards over the plateau for

◄ The screes of Beinn Dearg Mhór

about 200m, ignoring fenceposts that lead along the east ridge. Descend steeply SSE over worn scree to Bealach na Sgairde. Climb the scree of Beinn Dearg Mhór, more an exercise in balance than of momentum. The difficult section is soon passed before one final push along the arête to the summit. Descend southwest by a good path to Bealach Mosgaraidh, and follow the ridge to the top of Beinn Dearg Mheadhonach (GR515271) (4h). Drop northwest by a zigzag path to the flat ridge of Druim na Ruaige. This provides easy walking to a small cairned knoll. The path then drops more steeply and crosses boggy ground towards the Allt Daraich. Cross a stile to rejoin the ravine and return to the start (5h).

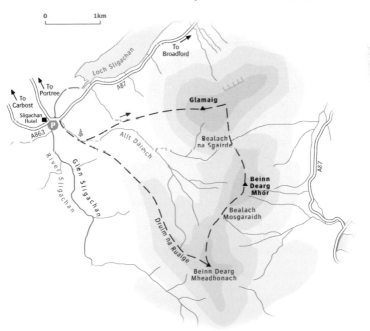

No two of the islands between the Mull of Kintyre and Skye have the same character. Islay is dominated by rolling moorland which supplies the peat for the island's many celebrated whisky distilleries. Its twin, Jura, is harsher and more remote. Mull is the wildlife-lover's paradise and has an unusual topography, with many long peninsulas leading into a high central massif. The Small Isles include Rum, managed by Scottish Natural Heritage, and Eigg, whose unusual profile can be distinguished from anywhere on the coast. Good ferry services run to all of the islands, but seadogs may choose to make their own way. The tidal flows between the islands can make for high adventure.

This section contains a rough route over the moorland of Islay and a long and challenging excursion to climb the three Paps of Jura. There are four routes on Mull: one ascends the sleeping giant of Ben More; another tackles the hills behind Craignure; an entertaining circuit follows the craggy coastline of Ardmeanach; and a final walk climbs the hills near Loch Buie. On the Small Isles, there is an ascent of An Sgùrr on Eigg and two circuits on Rum: one takes the hidden western peaks and the other scrambles over the charismatic Cuillin of Rum.

The Inner Hebrides

A taste of Islay

Glas Bheinn (472m),
Beinn Bheigier (491m)

Walk time 5h20 Height gain 800m
Distance 16km OS Map Landranger 60

An adventurous trek along wonderful coastline with rough mountain walking. Sharp navigation required in parts.

Start at the end of the minor road at Claggain Bay, 9km northeast of Ardbeg (GR462536). (Parking on the verge by the bay, but the journey from Port Ellen pier also makes a fine bike ride.) Cross the bridge over the Claggain River and head north along the private road, passing through two gates to reach the holiday cottage at Ardtalla. Pass this on the left side through another two gates, and traverse a grassy field to reach a small burn. Cross this by a bridge hidden in the gorse, then trend westwards to reach a gate after 50m. Pass through the gate, and follow the boggy track beyond. After about 200m the track forks: take the right fork to a gate after 20m. Pass through this gate and gain a little height before dropping down. Continue northwards on grassy tracks for 2km: this can be slippery but gives a good panorama of the sea as you approach the abandoned house at Proaig. Cross the burn by an iron girder before the old dwelling and 100m from the shore. Bear west from the house to find a grassy track which leads steeply uphill. It then turns northwest and slowly gains height, giving rough walking over folds and troughs. Higher up this

Chasing Cows
Will be our Fate
If you do not
Close this Gate

becomes a good bumpy ridge with a mixture of rock and heather. Follow this to the top of Glas Bheinn and its summit cairns (GR429592) (3h). Descend south past tiers of quartz which overlook a number of lochans to the west. Bear slightly west before following a ridge towards Am Màm, where the terrain begins to rise in a series of interlocking knolls. Trend southwest to avoid the scree and gain the west ridge of Beinn Bheigier. Climb steeply up heather to reach the summit trig point. Follow the ridge ESE over several knolls to reach the south summit, where two series of cairns begin. A more obvious line of cairns turns west, and a less frequently marked line bears southwards. Follow the latter to drop to lower ground, and then bear southeast to reach the corner of a fence. Continue southeast over rough ground, keeping the fence on the left until an older fence intersects at a solar panel after 500m. Cross this fence by a gate about 150m to the south to reach a track. Follow the track past a fenced clump of trees to reach the bridge over the Claggain River (5h20).

Geese, peat and whisky

One of the foremost ornithological sites in Europe, Islay's mild winter climate supports over 12,000 white-fronted geese (over a quarter of the world's population) and more than 30,000 barnacle geese. Their peat-bog habitat is also essential, however, to the island's famous whisky industry, and conservationists have in the past been in dispute with the farmers – although compromise has been reached in several important sites.

◂ On the way to Ardtalla from Claggain Bay

The Paps of Jura

Beinn Shiantaidh (757m),
Beinn an Oir Ⓖ (785m),
Beinn a'Chaolais (733m)

Walk time 8h40 Height gain 1600m
Distance 22km OS Map Landranger 61

A demanding trek to conquer an iconic trio: plenty of rough bog and steep scree, with few landmarks to guide.

Start in Craighouse (GR526674). (The village is served by regular buses from Feolin Pier, and ferries operate hourly from Port Askaig to Feolin.) Walk north along the main road to leave the village along the shoreline. After 5km, the road comes to the Three Arched Bridge over the Corran River. (Additional parking here.) Descend on the northwest side of the bridge to a stile. Cross the stile and head upstream, following a mix of tracks and rough ground with boggy stretches. After about 2km, cross to the opposite bank and trend northwest over complex slopes of heather and grass. These

gain gradual height, but the terrain is hard going. Make towards the bealach between Beinn Shiantaidh and Corra Bheinn, which is scored with a deep trench. From this point, the ground is much firmer. Climb the blunt southeast rib of Beinn Shiantaidh over heather and scree to reach the summit ridge. This is easily followed to the cairn on the west side of the peak. Drop due west: a pronounced ridge begins your descent but after a while loses definition in mounds of scree before steepening. Avoid low buttresses to reach easier ground and the wide bealach before Beinn an Oir. Start up the east face: in the lower part, a northward trending ramp helps you to gain easy height. Where this ends, continue straight up to gain the summit ridge and two old enclosures. Turn south to reach the summit and trig point (GR498749) (4h40). Descend the south ridge: this is exposed at first with some steep cliffs on the west side and provides an entertaining way down over

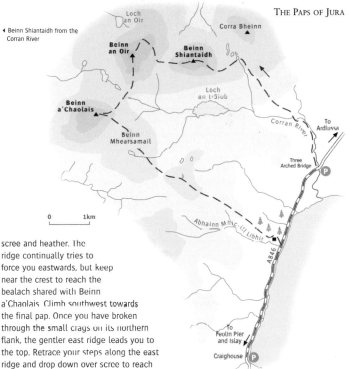

◄ Beinn Shiantaidh from the Corran River

scree and heather. The ridge continually tries to force you eastwards, but keep near the crest to reach the bealach shared with Beinn a'Chaolais. Climb southwest towards the final pap. Once you have broken through the small crags on its northern flank, the gentler east ridge leads you to the top. Retrace your steps along the east ridge and drop down over scree to reach the bealach. A direct climb takes you to the top of Beinn Mhearsamail, a small knoll; now descend southeast to boggier terrain. A grassy track winds its way southeast from here, diverging and reforming through featureless terrain, before eventually taking you close to the Abhainn Mhic-ill Libhir. The track reaches the south end of the Jura Forest, where a gate leads to a gravel track. Follow this through a leafy estate and down to the road to return to the start (8h40).

Orwell and Barnhill

In 1946 George Orwell moved to Barnhill in the north of Jura to aid his recovery from tuberculosis. Although he died from his condition within five years, he could have been gone sooner: he was lucky to survive an encounter with the Corryvreckan, the notorious area of water just off Jura's northern tip classed as unnavigable by the Royal Navy. Fortunately he made it safely back to Barnhill to finish writing *1984*.

Craignure of Mull

Dun da Ghaoithe Ⓖ (766m)

Walk time **6h** Height gain **800m**
Distance **17km** OS Map **Landranger 49**

**High corries, fine rocky ridges and good
tracks make this a varied walk. This
route can be combined with a tour of
Torosay Castle and gardens: the weary
can complete the last stretch by rail.**

Start from the ferry pier in Craignure
(GR718372). Walk 600m northwest along
the road for Tobermory, and turn left into
Scallastle Forest just before the Isle of Mull
Hotel. A gate at the plantation car park
leads to a gravel path through the trees.
Follow this path as it winds through new
and harvested forest with occasional
interpretive signs. At a junction after 1.5km,
take the right fork to drop down to the
Scallastle River. Cross the river by the
wooden bridge and, rather than follow a
gravel track upriver, turn right along a
fainter path to soon reach a gate. Pass
through the gate and bear west over
boggier ground, keeping between the fence
on your left and the Allt an Dubh-choire to
the right. Higher up, another fence traverses
the hillside. Cross this by a gate next to the
burn, below a small waterfall. Ford the burn
here, and climb westwards to join the
grassy ridge of Beinn Chreagach. Follow this
ridge southwest – it becomes firmer and
rockier above Coire na Circe – to reach the
summit of Dun da Ghaoithe (GR672362)

(3h). Descend south and climb again to reach Mainnir nam Fiadh, a sister top. Drop down along the bumps and dips of the east ridge to arrive at a communications complex, two huge masts with dishes and barbed wire. Beyond is a wide track that leads to a similar installation further down the ridge. Follow the track to the bird of prey centre, and down to the road. Turn left towards Craignure and follow the main road for about 300m. To avoid more road walking, follow signs on the right that lead you to Torosay Castle. If you have time, the house and gardens are well worth a visit. After your tour, make your way alongside the Mull Rail, Scotland's only island passenger railway, or hop on the train for the 2km journey back to Craignure (6h).

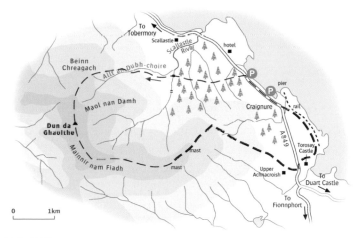

To the lighthouse

Lismore Lighthouse on Eilean Musdile in the Sound of Mull was built in 1833 by Robert Stevenson, Robert Louis Stevenson's grandfather. Automated in 1965, the beacon flashes every 10 seconds and has a nominal range of 19 miles. Near the lighthouse is Lady's Rock, so called because Lachlan Cattanach, a Maclean of Duart, decided to maroon his wife here in 1527 because she could not provide him with an heir. Unfortunately for Lachlan, she was soon rescued by passing fishermen and years later he was found murdered in his bed.

◀ Lismore Lighthouse from the ferry between Oban and Craignure

Loch Buie pilgrimage

Creach Beinn (698m)

Walk time 4h20 Height gain 800m
Distance 11km OS Map Landranger 49

**A half-day walk over mixed terrain
requiring good navigation. This route is
approached from the head of Loch Buie.
Access is also possible from Glen More
to the north.**

Start from Lochbuie, home to the ruined
Moy Castle, at a bridge over the Abhainn
a'Chaiginn Mhóir (GR615255). (Limited
parking here.) A gate on the east side of the
bridge gives access to a path that leads
north along the Gleann a'Chaiginn Mhóir.
This shortly passes a ruin and, after about
300m, snakes up over a mound. The path is

easily lost here but continues about 100m
east of the burn. Climb gently up the glen:
just past a waterfall the terrain levels out.
Here, the path becomes fainter as it crosses
the bog and continues on the west side of
the glen, over the watershed and down to
Loch Airdeglais. At the foot of this loch,
leave the path to climb first east and then
northeast over rough ground and along a
steep-sided burn. This soon reaches a
natural bowl with broken crags ahead. Cross
the flatter ground to gain the north end of
the rocks. Climb ESE over complex terrain
with many rocky steps to the top of Beinn
Fhada and its tiny summit lochans. Descend
southwest past a line of outcrops to a
boggy bealach. Climb southeast along a

◄ Loch Buie from Creach Beinn

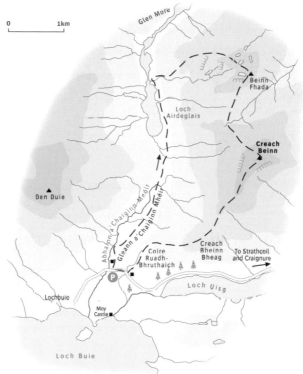

0   1km

blunt ridge over grass and scree to the rocky summit of Creach Beinn (GR643276) (3h20). Descend via the southwest ridge: this is good fun and mostly easy with occasional steeper sections. When the ridge flattens out, don't be tricked westwards off the ridge but continue to Creach Bheinn

Bheag and follow the spur WSW for a further 1km beyond. Much lower down, where the ridge bucks and dips, it is best to descend southwest into Coire Ruadh-Bhruthaich. Aim just to the west of the house: hummocky slopes bring you onto the road close to the start (4h20).

Ben More of Mull

Beinn Fhada (702m), **Ben More** Ⓜ(966m)

Walk time 6h20 Height gain 1200m
Distance 14km OS Map Landranger 48

This strenuous route starts by a great waterfall to climb several ridges before a scramble on Ben More. Exposed ridges and tricky navigation, often in mist, add to the adventure.

Start at a bridge over the Scarisdale River on the B8035, 5km southwest of Gruline (GR517375). (Limited parking at points along this road: do not block passing places.) From the east side of the bridge, cross boggy ground close to the north bank of the Scarisdale River. This soon steepens, to give intimidating views into the ravine which ends higher up at a waterfall. Cross the river just above the waterfall with ease, and start to climb southeast over the increasingly rocky terrain that leads to the summit of Beinn nan Gabhar. Descend southwards to a bealach and begin a curving ascent over grass to the top of Beinn Fhada: the summit is a steep-sided rocky knoll (GR540349) (2h40). [Escape: descend the northwest ridge of Beinn Fhada. This is steep to start, with another

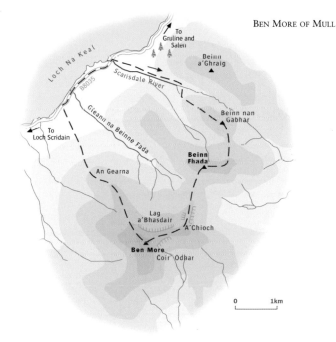

short tricky section after 500m.] Descend south to a bealach and begin to climb A'Chioch, a satellite peak of Ben More: as the ground steepens steadily it provides an entertaining scramble without any major difficulties. Drop to a bealach and continue along the high and steep-sided east ridge. This offers some exposure as the apex is narrow. Eventually, your efforts are rewarded by the summit and trig point of Ben More (GR525330) (4h40). To lose height quickly, descend northwest over the scree-covered slopes high above Lag a'Bhasdair. The incline eases towards An Gearna. Continue northwards over heather to arrive at the coast not far from the start (6h20).

Bagging

Ben More, the 'big mountain' of Mull, is the only island Munro (peak over 914m/3000ft) outside of Skye. Sir Hugh Munro was the first to list and attempt to climb all of these peaks although he never realised his ambition, failing in his second attempt to conquer the Inaccessible Pinnacle in 1915 at the age of 60. Today, the Scottish Mountaineering Club records 284 Munros and 'bagging' them all is the great aspiration for some.

◀ Ben More from the peaks of Ardmeanach

The Ardmeanach Peninsula

Beinn na Sreine (521m)

Walk time **5h40** Height gain **800m**
Distance **15km** OS Map Landranger 48

The Ardmeanach peninsula enjoys clear weather when higher peaks are in mist. This route starts by a waterfall, climbs several hills on rough ground and returns by a good track. It overlooks The Wilderness, an area of outstanding natural beauty.

Start at the end of the public road above Kilfinichen Bay and the start of a track to Burg (GR478275). (Limited parking.) Walk west along the track and take the right fork at a junction after 500m. Continue past the Tiroran Old School and through a short section of forest. At a bend in the track,

roughly 500m west of the schoolhouse, two burns cascade from the north. Leave the track and follow the burn on the right, climbing steeply north. Where the burn ends in level ground, continue north over a steep knoll to flatter rocky ground. This leads to the top of Maol Mheadhonach and a cairn. Walk NNW over undulating but fairly firm ground, bypassing or ascending a small knoll before climbing to the top of Beinn na Sreine (GR456304) (2h20). This summit is set above a steep escarpment that gives views of the Isle of Ulva, the Ross of Mull, Iona and Ben More. Walk easily west, past low crags and a lochan, to Fionna Mhàm. From this point, the ridge drops to a boggy low point scored with dykes. Turn southwards to climb Creach Bheinn: this

involves ascending or avoiding a knoll before several rocky steps lead west to the summit and trig point, which looks out across The Wilderness and the rough coast. Descend south, keeping a lochan to the west, and cross an old fence before friendly slopes and short climbs lead to Bearraich, the final top. Drop northeast from the summit to pick up the start of a burn just to the south of a fence marking the National Trust for Scotland boundary. Sheep trails to the right of the burn lead easily down to a kink in the fence before a grassy knoll. Keep left of the knoll and head for a gap in the corner of an old wall. Pass through the gap, and head straight over bracken slopes to reach the track from Burg. Follow this track for 5km to the start (5h40).

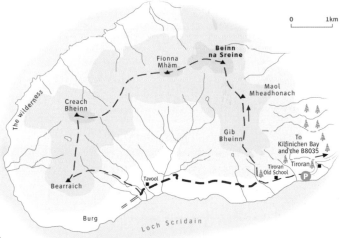

Iona

A kilometre off the southwest tip of Mull, Iona is an important centre for pilgrimage and retreat for Christians of all denominations from all over the world. St Columba landed here in 563 and founded a religious establishment which, although frequently pillaged and desecrated by Norsemen, grew over the centuries as a place of special spiritual significance. It is also the burial place of 48 Scottish, eight Norwegian and four Irish kings as well as, more recently, John Smith, leader of the Labour Party and keen hillwalker.

◀ Kilfinichen Bay

A scramble on Eigg

An Sgùrr (393m)

Walk time **3h20** Height gain **400m**
Distance **9km** OS Map **Landranger 39**

A short scramble on the charismatic 'Notch' of Eigg, which can be completed between the arrival and departure of the ferry from Mallaig or Arisaig.

Start from the ferry pier in Galmisdale (GR486837). Walk along the road past the tearoom, and turn left along the track at the first junction. Follow it westwards as it winds its way up through woodland and past a pink house. Bear left at the next junction to arrive at a gate into open country. Go through the gate and follow the track to a large red and white house: walk between the house and a shed on the right to reach another gate with a track beyond. Turn left to follow this new track for 80m to a cairn and path on the right. The path climbs gently across moorland towards the cliffs of An Sgùrr, passing more cairns en route. After reaching a high point, the path passes the mountain on its northern side, trending under high crags for about 500m. Climb south at the first easy breach in the cliffs, rising through a natural gully to reach the main ridge. Some easy moves of scrambling begin the ascent east along the

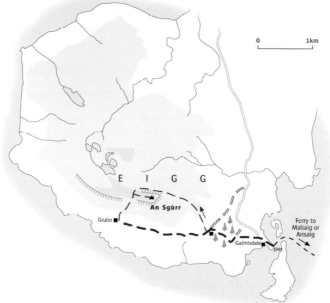

ridge. After these, the terrain undulates over interesting features and knolls to reach the trig point which is set close to the edge of the main rockface (GR463847) (2h). To descend, retrace your steps, including the first scrambling moves, but stay on the ridge. Descend to the south, following a gully with spectacular hexagonal rock formations for about 30m until it steepens.

Now take the heather-covered rake to the right until there is an easy way back into the gully. Lower down, make your way through bracken to reach a good grassy track near the cottage of Grulin, which is set amongst huge boulders. Take the track eastwards to meet the red and white house, and return to the pier (3h20).

Minke's whales

Minke whale are often seen around Eigg's coastal waters, especially between July and September. They are the smallest of the baleen (filter-feeding) whales and have distinctive pointed snouts, relatively short flippers and light underbellies. They take their name from an infamous Norwegian whaler who regularly broke the rules about what he could kill. All small whales became known as 'Minke's whales', but the name stuck with this one.

◄ Looking out to Muck from Grulin on Eigg

77

The Cuillin of Rum

Sgùrr nan Gillean (764m),
Ainshval ⓖ (781m), **Askival** ⓖ (812m)

Walk time **8h** Height gain **1400m**
Distance **21km** OS Map Landranger 39

A strenuous circuit of Rum's high peaks, which requires good mountain skills. An overnight stop is an option.

Start from the Reserve Office just south of Kinloch Castle (GR403993). (Leave route card in the box.) Walk southeast on the track from the house, passing white gates after 150m. Watch for the Pony Path marked for Dibidil, 50m beyond. This leads you in zigzags up the hill before levelling out (occasionally boggy) for some distance along the coast. On turning the south ridge of Beinn nan Stac, the path leads you above steep slopes with the bothy of Dibidil set at the foot of a deep glen ahead. Regain the path above the bothy and follow it southwards, gaining gradual height. After about 1km, where it begins to descend, leave the path to climb undulating slopes northwest. Higher up, the ground steepens: follow grassy runnels through broken crags to reach the easier terrain that leads to the summit of Sgùrr nan Gillean (GR382931) (4h20). Follow the ridge northwest and climb to a second top. This has an exposed and steep northeast ridge which provides easy scrambling, mostly taken on the west side, to reach a bealach. A short grassy climb takes you to the summit of Ainshval.

Walk about 30m northwest and leave the ridge by descending north into a bowl of scree and broken rock just below and to the east side of the steep north ridge. A path descends diagonally to gain a level area about halfway down. From this point, descend northwest, keeping to the right side of a slope of scree and boulders, effectively avoiding the main ridge on the west side. This leads down to Bealach an Fhuarain. Climb northwards, avoiding the first broken buttress on the right, to gain a scree runnel. Higher up, low crags can be avoided on the east to reach the double-headed summit of Trollaval. Descend by the east ridge: early difficulties can be eased by keeping to the north side of the crest to reach Bealach an Oir. [Escape: descend north into Atlantic Corrie and cross to Bealach Bairc-mheall.] Climb eastwards to gain the summit of Askival (GR393952) (6h). Descend north to gain a scree-covered platform. The north ridge is steep and should be treated with care. Keep to the east side, following a path that drops down over short grassy steps, increasing distance from the crest. Traverse to rejoin the ridge below the Askival Pinnacle. (The ridge direct requires rock-climbing and has seen recent rockfall.) Drop easily to the bealach

and climb through tiers of broken rock to reach the summit of Hallival. Descend the northwest ridge over scree and crags to gain flatter ground. Cross slippery scree to gain Bealach Baire-mheall. Descend northwards over rough ground into Coire Dubh. Lower down, go through a gate in a fence to an excellent path that leads into the Kinloch Estate. Shortly after passing a wall, take a right fork into the castle grounds close to the start (8h).

◄ Trollaval from Askival

79

Peaks of the West

Ard Nev (556m), **Orval** (571m)

Walk time **6h** Height gain **700m**
Distance **18km** OS Map Landranger 39

A rewarding route on easy paths from Kinloch Castle. Good alternative if weather is too poor for the Rum Cuillin.

Start from Kinloch Castle (GR401996). Take the track north for 150m to the crossroads, turn left and follow an excellent stony track westwards along Kinloch Glen, passing through a gate with views of the waterfall. At a junction after 3km, take the left fork to start climbing southwest, crossing two bridges. About 2km after the second bridge, where old trees stumps and fenceposts litter the moor to the west, leave the track and climb southwest. Follow a streambed, passing an old shelter towards a grassy knoll topped by a small tor. This gains the main ridge of Ard Nev: bear north and climb the spur, passing a small lochan and ascending many rounded and interlocking bumps to reach the summit (GR346986) (3h). Descend northwest along the ridge to a prominent bealach, where

Orval presents its craggy eastern corrie. Climb west, avoiding the scree on the right and zigzagging with ease between small crags to reach easy ground on the plateau. The true summit of Orval is a small detour west. Descend NNE along a folding and ill-defined spur. The steepening slopes to Bealach a'Bhraigh Bhig are best negotiated slightly on the east side. A path winds down to the boggy reaches of the Monadh Mhiltich and meets the original track at the bridge. Return to the castle (6h).

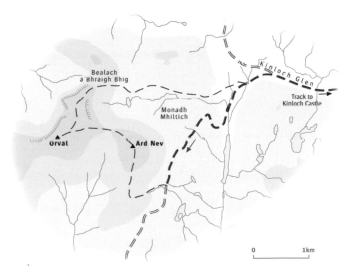

Kinloch Castle

Lancastrian textile magnate Sir George Bullough began building Kinloch Castle in 1897 and on its completion filled it with souvenirs gathered on his international travels. The privacy the castle afforded Sir George also meant that he was able to throw parties which would have raised more than a few eyebrows elsewhere. Today the castle is in the care of Scottish Natural Heritage and still contains a great many bizarre artefacts.

◀ Rum from Coire a'Ghrunnda on Skye

At no more than twenty miles long and ten miles wide, Arran is often described as 'Scotland in miniature' as it has a landscape which changes dramatically as the visitor journeys on the twisting road around the island. Fine beaches with a backdrop of low-lying, gently rolling hills in the south contrast with the granite crags and high peaks to the north. An efficient public transport system links with the regular ferries that arrive at and depart from Brodick.

All of the routes in this section are in the mountainous north, and the access points can be reached by bus. There are two interlocking routes that start close to Brodick and walk along Glen Rosa to reach the high peaks: one of these involves some complex scrambling; the other is less technical. One circuit begins from Corrie and climbs Goatfell, the highest point on the island. Another route with some easy scrambling climbs over the Sleeping Warrior, reclining at the end of Glen Sannox.

Lochranza makes a good base for the routes in the north, and is the start point for an easier walk along three glens. The last excursion takes in the reclusive hills above the Kilbrannan Sound and the Mull of Kintyre.

The Isle of Arran

Peaks of Glen Rosa

Beinn Tarsuinn (826m),
Beinn Nuis (792m)

Walk time 5h40 Height gain 800m
Distance 16km OS Map Explorer 361

A great ridge walk with an exciting approach. Those with climbing skills may want to extend this route to include A'Chir and Cir Mhór (see the next walk: Scramble on A'Chir).

Start at the end of the public road and campsite in Glen Rosa, easily reached on foot from Brodick (GR001376). Walk northwest along the track through the glen. After about 1km, this becomes a path and later bridges the Garbh Allt. Cross over, and immediately take the lesser path which leads steeply west along the burn: this enters and exits a fenced area where the path has been upgraded. Continue alongside the water above the upper gate to the point where two burns meet. Accompany the northern one to another fence with a stile. Beyond the stile, follow a path to cross the water in a narrow ravine. Cross the flat ground of Coire a'Bhradain

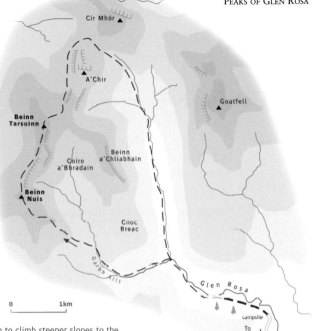

and begin to climb steeper slopes to the eastern corrie of Beinn Nuis. Wide slabs and perched boulders lead to the summit (GR955399) (3h). Drop northwards to a bealach and then continue to the summit of Beinn Tarsuinn. Descend northeast, weaving through crags and boulders. After dropping about 150m and passing over a short slippery slab, you reach a set of large rounded boulders. [Escape: Cross the ridge and descend southeast. A good path leads over Beinn a'Chliabhain and back to the start.] Continue the descent northwards to the bealach. The traverse of A'Chir demands good scrambling skills and considerable

nerve: the route avoids this peak by taking an obvious traversing path on the western slopes, passing through a boulderfield. After about 1km, the path reaches the ridge. Follow the main ridge for about 300m to a prominent bealach shared with Cir Mhór. Descend by a good path to Fionn Choire and continue southeast into Glen Rosa. Return along this glen to the start (5h40).

◄ Glen Rosa and Cir Mhór

85

Scramble on A'Chir

A'Chir (720m), **Cir Mhór** ⓒ (799m)

Walk time **6h** Height gain **800m**
Distance **16km** OS Map **Explorer 361**

A winding route over two high and rocky peaks. Difficult scrambling, exposure and navigation, and some climbing (a rope is recommended) with the hardest moves in descent, make this very tricky in wet or winter conditions.

Start at the end of the public road and campsite in Glen Rosa, easily reached on foot from Brodick (GR001376). Walk northwest along the track through the glen. After about 1km, this becomes a path and later bridges the Garbh Allt. Cross over, and

immediately take the lesser path which leads steeply west along the burn: this enters and exits a fenced area where the path has been upgraded. Leave the water on exiting the fenced area and bear northwest, aiming for the small knoll of Cnoc Breac. This leads to a good ridge on the east side of Coire a'Bhradain and on to the top of Beinn a'Chliabhain. Descend to a bealach with views of the steep corries of Beinn Tarsuinn and A'Chir. Climb northwest, keeping to the south area of the ridge, to reach the northeast ridge of Beinn Tarsuinn. Continue the descent northwards to the bealach shared with A'Chir and start to gain height along the ridge. At a notch with an overhanging wall on the corrie side, begin a meandering scramble over slabs, keeping just to the west side of the apex to reach a rocky knoll below the top. A short descent from here requires 5m of climbing down a corner to easy ground. Climb through a gully to the airy summit (GR966422) (3h). Descend west with care: the ridge is very exposed with unforgiving cliffs, particularly to the north. Multiple steps over slabs and bulges lead to a very exposed gap above a rock window: this may be the Bad Step but the difficulties are not yet over. The next part of the ridge is fairly level but ends in overhanging cliffs: walk about halfway between the gap and the cliffs to find a sneaky descent on the east side. Climb down a short wall using a prominent flake to reach a hidden grassy rake that runs horizontally north. This ledge becomes encased as you continue and constricts to give a final awkward move before you reach easy ground below the cliffs. A small final tower is comparatively easy and no further difficulties remain in descent to gain the bealach above Fionn Choire. [Escape: descend easily east by a good path into Glen Rosa.] Climb easily northeast to the summit of Cir Mhór at the centre of the range. This has many great rockfaces: descend with care along the east ridge. After some initial difficulties, the terrain eases and the ridge is followed by a good path down to The Saddle. Descend due south from this bealach by a path into Glen Rosa and back to the start (6h).

◄ Cir Mhór from A'Chir

Goatfell

Goatfell ⓒ (874m)

Walk time **4h20** Height gain **1000m**
Distance **10km** OS Map **Explorer 361**

**An entertaining route over the highest
peak on Arran, with scrambling options
and a winding return.**

Start at the track leading to High Corrie
and waymarked for Goatfell, south of the
village hall at the south end of Corrie
(GR026422). Walk up the track and take the
left fork after 400m. Tarmac soon leads to
gravel after which a signposted path follows
the edge of the plantation to the north,
keeping close to the Corrie Burn. Cross a
stile out onto open ground and ascend
steep slopes by the waterfall, crossing
another stile to flatter, easier terrain. The
path divides soon after a cairn: take the left
fork to cross the burn and start to climb
southwest to Meall Breac. This ridge rises
gradually before it begins to steepen at an
intersection of paths. Continue to gain
height through boulders, avoiding the
steeper rocky ground near the top by
trending left to reach the summit of
Goatfell (GR991415) (2h40). Descend
northwards over large boulders to the three
towers of Stacach. These can be tackled
directly, with some scrambling in ascent
and descent, or avoided completely by a
path that keeps to the east side of the
ridge. It is one short scramble to the
summit of North Goatfell. Make sure you
descend northeast over easy terrain to a
bealach. [Variant: North Goatfell can be

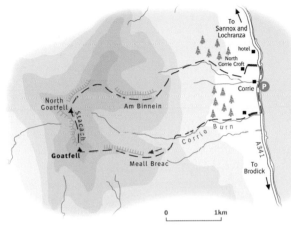

avoided completely by turning it on the east side.] [Escape: from the bealach, descend southeast over grass into Coire Lan, keeping north of the burn. This rejoins the main path.] Climb NNE over scree and around boulders to reach Mullach Buidhe, which has several tops. From the first top trend ESE, descending gradually. A narrow path takes the crest of Am Binnein over knolls with granite block. A cross adorns a final knoll on the ridge. Descend easily by a path to the northeast. Further down, where the spur loses definition, head into the corrie and follow the burn over rough ground until it levels out. When you see a stile and fence, cross the burn, climb the stile and follow the vague path beyond: this keeps close to the burn to reach a plantation after about 400m. Now bear southeast by the burn, keeping the forest on your left, to reach a gate after 300m. Beyond the gate, negotiate rough ground for 100m. From here, a good path overlooking the burn (now a ravine) can be followed to an intersection. Turn left to avoid the private gardens straight ahead, and take a path on the right after 200m: this leads through bracken to North Corrie Croft where a track takes you back to the village (4h20).

Tintin on Arran

Fans of Tintin will be interested to know that Arran inspired *The Black Island*, the only one of Hergé's books to feature the boy reporter wearing a kilt. With his faithful terrier Snowy and Captain Haddock, a foul-mouthed sailor, Tintin tracks down a criminal gang to Lochranza Castle and discovers the true identity of 'The Beast' within. Meticulous in his research, George Remy (Hergé) visited Arran to make sketches before creating the adventure, first published in 1938.

◀ Bird life on the summit of Goatfell

The Warrior and the Witch

Caisteal Abhail © (859m)

Walk time **5h** Height gain **900m**
Distance **10km** OS Map Explorer 361

A fine horseshoe ridge, which involves complex terrain with plenty of exposure and some tricky sections. Scrambling and navigation skills are essential.

Start at the bridge and large car park 2.5km northwest of Sannox (GR011461). A good path leads west along North Glen Sannox to reach a stile and forest beyond. The path becomes boggy as it threads through the trees and along the burn, but soon leaves the plantation by another stile. Shortly after, cross the burn to the north side. Bear northwest over awkward slopes to gain flat ground, and then steeply south to tackle the blunt ridge of Sail an Im on a faint gravel path. The ridge takes you over Creag Dhubh and onto Carn Mór, with steep crags to the east. Continue along the corrie

rim towards Caisteal Abhail, passing a number of tors, to reach complex and indented ground with folds and steep buttresses. The summit is recognisable with a large west-facing crag, like a castle: find the exposed path that traverses a short way above the northern corrie to a point just east of the summit: from here it is a short scramble to the top of Caisteal Abhail (GR969443) (3h). Descend and follow the crest of the east ridge. This involves some tricky steps, although most difficulties can be minimised by variations on the south side. The ridge leads to two rocky knolls: the first can be climbed through, but the second is a high tower which should be taken on the south. A steep descent over loose gravel follows, leading to the seemingly impassable notch before Ceum na Caillich (known as the Witches' Step). Descend scree and gravel on the north side for about 20m in height until you are just

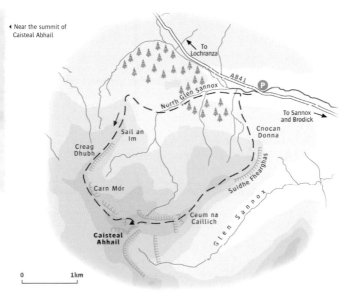

◀ Near the summit of
Caisteal Abhail

0   1km

past a triangular slab in the centre of the gully. A path on the right climbs a short corner to gain an easy terrace above. This traverses easier ground to emerge on the ridge on the far side of Ceum na Caillich. [Variant: rock-climbers may wish to climb directly from the notch.] Continue northeast with ease, and climb slightly to a small knoll. The ridge leads to Suidhe Fhearghas with its steep eastern cliffs, where the path turns northwest and cuts steeply down. Lower still, a few awkward slabs take you to the boggy Cnocan Donna. Descend north over heathery slopes from here to reach North Glen Sannox. Pick up the original path to the start (5h).

Warriors and spiders

For resembling a reclining soldier in profile, Arran's shapely central peaks are known collectively as the Sleeping Warrior. The other warrior associated with the island is Robert the Bruce who is said to have encountered the spider which inspired him to 'try, try, and try again' in a cave near Blackwaterfoot. There are other caves around Scotland, however, that claim the legend, including one in a caravan park in Dumfries.

To the Twelve Apostles

Beinn Bhreac (575m)

Walk time 5h20 Height gain 600m
Distance 14km OS Map Landranger 69

**An uncomplicated route through three
scenic glens and up one peak that looks
to the Glen Rosa mountains.**

Start in the village of Lochranza
(GR933504). Walk along the road to the
southeast end of the village. Continue until
just past the distillery and immediately
before the humpback bridge, then take the
grassy track signposted for the Sleeping
Warrior on the south side of the road. This
soon becomes a path and rises above a
hidden waterfall. The wide Gleann Easan
Biorach opens up beyond: this gives good
walking, although the path can be boggy
over the next 1km. Higher up, the route
improves as it climbs to reach the miniature
Loch na Davie with great views of Beinn
Tarsuinn. Continue along the path until it
turns west to skirt the flanks of Beinn
Bhreac after 500m. At this point, leave the
main path and bear northwest to follow the
rocky ridge to the summit of Beinn Bhreac
(GR943456) (3h). Descend northwest to
flatter terrain, keeping the tor-ringed Beinn

Bhiorach on your right. Now drop westwards over easy grass slopes to reach an excellent path into the National Nature Reserve of Gleann Diomhan. The path keeps to the right hand side of a fence as it descends northwards into Glen Catacol. Further down, you will meet another path: follow this downstream to reach a stile which gives access to the road by a bridge. Turn right to the hotel at Catacol and the Twelve Apostles. Follow the road or seashore round the headland and back to Lochranza (5h20).

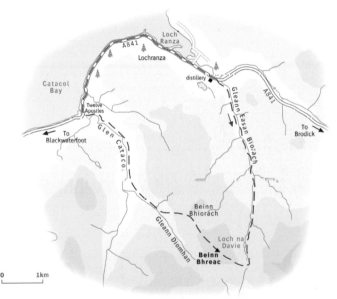

The Catacol Apostles

The twelve identical white cottages on the seafront at Catacol were built by the Duke of Hamilton to house the crofters of Abhainn Bheag who had been displaced by sheep. At first the crofters refused to live in them and the cottages, known also as 'the hungry row', lay empty for two years before being let.

◀ Lower Glen Catacol

Hills of Kilbrannan Sound

Beinn Breac (711m),
Beinn Bharrain (721m)

Walk time 5h40 Height gain 900m
Distance 14km OS Map Landranger 69

An entertaining walk over two rocky peaks which are often out of cloud when the main massif on Arran is hidden. The return involves some tricky navigation.

Start in Pirnmill on the west coast of the island (GR872443). Walk north along the coastline for 2.5km to reach houses at Mid Thunderguy. Wind up through the houses on the track for Coirein Lochain. Behind the last bungalow, two gates lead out on to open ground. Take the gate on the right and start to climb grassy slopes, diverging slightly from a fence that you keep on your

left to reach a more defined path. This leads though bracken to a stile: cross this to follow the sometimes boggy path ahead, fording a burn twice while accompanying it upstream. After passing two large cairns, you will come to the shores of Coire Fhionn Lochan. Cross the outlet burn and follow the good path along the north bank of the loch. Climb to a slab-covered bealach just south of Meall Bhig. At the first cairn on the bealach, bear south to ascend steep slopes. These relent and lead over a short knoll before the final push to the summit of Beinn Bhreac. Descend SSE along the excellent ridge to a prominent bealach. Climb southwest to reach the trig point and summit of Beinn Bharrain (GR902427) (4h). Follow the ridge, dotted with tors and slabs,